DC

WITHDRAWN

Oil's First Century

Papers Given at the Centennial Seminar on the History of the Petroleum Industry

Harvard Business School
November 13–14, 1959

PUBLISHED BY THE HARVARD GRADUATE
SCHOOL OF BUSINESS ADMINISTRATION

COMPILED AND EDITED BY THE STAFF
OF THE BUSINESS HISTORY REVIEW

SEMINAR SPONSORS

ATLANTIC REFINING COMPANY

CONTINENTAL OIL COMPANY

ETHYL CORPORATION

GULF OIL CORPORATION

JENNEY MANUFACTURING COMPANY

SOCONY MOBIL OIL COMPANY

STANDARD OIL COMPANY OF CALIFORNIA

STANDARD OIL COMPANY (INDIANA)

STANDARD OIL COMPANY (NEW JERSEY)

STANDARD OIL COMPANY (OHIO)

SHELL OIL COMPANY

SUN OIL COMPANY

TEXACO, INCORPORATED

CONTENTS

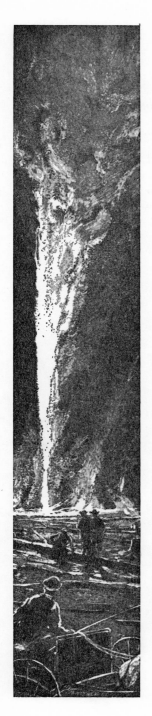

132128

C O N T E N T S

(continued)

Public Policy and the Petroleum Industry

FOREWORD

by Ralph W. Hidy

HARVARD BUSINESS SCHOOL

More research and writing have been done on the history of the oil industry than on any other, possibly excepting transportation. Historians have probed an unusually wide range of topics, including particular companies, individual executives, regional operations in the United States, development of regulation and critical analyses of regulatory measures, legal relations, integration, and operations in foreign nations. The flow of work continues, providing new insights into the evolution of this particular industry and also new data on such broad areas as the role of entrepreneurship in economic development, government-business relations, and conservation of natural resources. Some of the work has been critical of the industry and its leaders, and some has been favorable. Since the historian's job is neither to condemn nor to condone but to understand, it seemed worthwhile to bring students of oil history together with oilmen and government representatives for a mutual exchange of views on significant aspects of the industry's development. A collateral result of such a meeting, it was hoped, would be a better understanding by businessmen of what historians are trying to do and a clearer appreciation by academicians of the problems, motivations, and methods of businessmen. Industry-wide celebration of the centennial of the Drake well provided a suitable background and stimulus for such a conference. A number of corporations showed an active interest in the project and provided funds for its realization; without their aid, hereby gratefully acknowledged, the conference would not have been held nor this collection of essays seen the light of day. The response of those invited to give papers and share informally in the proceedings was equally prompt and enthusiastic.

On Friday, November 13, 1959, the seminar convened at the Harvard Business School. In the morning session R. J. Forbes presented evidence that the petroleum industry had already developed to a considerable extent in various parts of the world before Drake dramatically drilled his well at Titusville.

Kendall Beaton next gave a résumé of developments in North America before 1859, thus providing a good perspective for an evaluation of the actual significance of the Drake well as assessed in the next paper by Paul H. Giddens. On this section of the program, dealing with the foundations of the petroleum industry, historians led most of the discussion, the business representatives being content for the most part to listen.

In the first afternoon session the papers focussed on the oil industry's rapid move toward concentration and integration, with attendant problems and implications for the future patterns of development. Henrietta Larson analyzed some of the characteristic features and implications of the large-scale enterprise which emerged at an early state of industrial growth in the United States. Arthur Johnson then elaborated on some of the problems arising from concentration, ranging in his discussion from intra-industry frictions as a factor in the evolution of public policies to the impact of antitrust legislation and court decisions. Businessmen now began to contribute their ideas on the significance of the historical patterns emerging prior to World War I.

At the dinner meeting on Friday evening Wallace E. Pratt gave his views as to the value of business history in the search for oil. He gave a glimpse of the reasons why executives of Standard Oil Company (New Jersey) had thought it desirable to have a comprehensive, objective history of their firm, but he stressed the idea that historians should give more attention to decisions and actions connected with the exploration for and the recovery of raw petroleum.

The next day Harold Williamson analyzed the factors contributing to the appearance of a large number of firms in the industry after 1900 and pointed up the relation of this economic fact to the competitive pattern emerging before as well as after the dismemberment of the Standard Oil combination by court order in 1911. To illustrate the new kind of competition in the industry after 1920, Edmund P. Learned presented some of the results of his study of pricing patterns in Ohio, an intensive analysis illustrating the detailed workings of some of the broad market forces discussed in other papers. At the luncheon meeting John Enos summarized findings of his recent research, presenting a view of technological innovation in the cracking process as a part of the competitive pattern since 1913.

Papers given at the last session of the seminar resulted in lively discussion on the part of historians and businessmen alike. George S. Wolbert presented an historical brief for continued inclusion of pipelines in integrated oil companies. Ensuing discussion indicated that, though the "spectre of divorcement" was not yet dead, it was not as pressing as it once had been. Simon N. Whitney briefly analyzed changes in the industry under the Sherman Act, but, as befitting his status as a representative of a governmental regulatory agency, made no prophecies for the future. In the final paper by James W. Mackie and Stephen L. McDonald, however, there was a definite suggestion that conservation laws should be modified to take cognizance of the economics of the situation at the present time. Since the findings of the two authors are to be published elsewhere, in extenso, the paper has not been included in this volume, to its loss. The conference ended on a note strongly suggesting that representatives of the business and academic worlds had much to say to each other and that the ideas exchanged on the centennial of the Drake well, valuable in themselves, were but the beginning of a more constant and informed exchange that in future years might be developed to great mutual advantage.

Oil in Eastern Europe
1840-1859

by R. J. Forbes

AMSTERDAM

It may seem strange that we discuss in a
seminar held to commemorate the centenary
of Drake's successful oil well the development of the oil industry in Eastern Europe
in the two decades preceding it. For this
oil industry was not only remote in space
from Titusville, it did not feel its repercussions until several years later, when depots
for the imported American lamp oil and
lubricants were erected on the shores of the
Atlantic and the Mediterranean and when
drilling started at least in Galicia and Roumania, some 20 years after Drake's attempt
to tap the subsoil resources of oil. In fact
there was little contact between the American
oil industry and that in the Far East or in

Europe before the decade of 1880–1890, when the world petroleum industry began to take shape.[1]

Some doubt might be cast on the existence of a European petroleum industry before Drake, but however modest its extension was, we cannot deny that local centers were gradually extending their activities and probing the markets of a Europe, where, from 1840 onwards, the Industrial Revolution was gaining momentum. This European petroleum industry had slowly grown during many centuries.

We know that after the Dark Ages the classical tradition about petroleum and its products was never lost, but that doctors, pharmacists, geologists, and chemists discussed the substance, found new seepages, and analyzed crudes. And we also know that certain groups of seepages, the modest precursors of our oilfields, were in constant production from the Middle Ages onwards. For centuries crude was produced from the seepages at Wietze (Hannover, Germany); Pechelbron (Alsace); Béziers (Southern France); Agrigentum (Sicily); the Modena region in the Po Valley; Tegernsee (Southern Bavaria); Galicia; Roumania; and Baku. Of course production did not amount to much, but it was widely used locally as an illuminant, as a lubricant or cart grease, and as a remedy for cattle diseases. Very prominent was its medical use, backed by classical tradition, and the oil (sometimes distillates) from these different seepages competed heavily in the fairs and markets of Europe as recorded in a number of pamphlets, printed as far back as 1480.

Now the turn of the eighteenth century saw the birth of a powerful stimulus for the rise of a European petroleum industry, the birth of the new oil lamp. Argand's invention, copied and improved by a generation of inventors and manufacturers, had at last provided by around 1840 a variety of burners which could utilize many kinds of illuminants, though all of relatively low candle power. These Sinumbra lamps, or whatever other name they might bear, with their woven wicks, lamp glass, and very often with a device forcing the oil toward the flame, had little to fear from competition until the 1880's. Gas burned in fish-tail burners was no serious competitor until Auer von Welsbach invented the gas mantle in 1883. Nor was the electric arc light a serious economic competitor; electric bulbs were not produced until 1886! However, within the illuminant trade there was very serious

[1] Material for this paper was taken from R. J. Forbes, *Studies in Early Petroleum History* (Leiden, 1958), and R. J. Forbes, *More Studies in Early Petroleum History* (Leiden, 1959).

competition. Lamp oil was produced from cannel coal, notably in Scotland; from wood tar, mainly in Scandinavia; from lignite in Germany; and from shale in France and in Scotland. The tar industry marketed its "photogen" or "camphene" fractions and there were the traditional animal and vegetable oils like whale oil, rapeseed oil, linseed oil, etc., though the latter were gradually abandoned in favor of the cheaper mineral oils with lower viscosity and more standardized quality. All these industries were well established (some of them survived up to modern times) and produced great quantities of good lamp oil.

How were the local seepages of Europe to compete with such formidable opponents? It was, of course, well known that crude oil could be burned in primitive lamps. As far back as 1802 street lights in the Italian towns of Parma, Borgo San Donino, and Genoa used the crude of the Modena region. It was also common knowledge by 1840 that a much better illuminant could be distilled from crude, but here the European refiners were at a disadvantage when compared with their later Pennsylvanian colleagues. Whereas Pennsylvania can more or less be called a "one-crude-country" in those early days the European seepages yielded a large variety of crudes. Each of these had to be refined in a different way. We are all aware, for example, of the high aromatic content of many Roumanian crudes, which degraded Roumanian lamp oil to second quality until early in our century, when means were found to extract these aromatic components and produce a high-grade kerosene. Therefore we find that producing lamp oil from any given European crude was a trade secret, which could be lost and rediscovered. Joseph Hecker knew how to produce good kerosene from Galician crude in 1810, but the secret was lost as his business failed and Lukasiewicz had to discover the art all over again in 1850! Such vagueries were dispelled by 1880 when the basic facts of organic chemistry and the composition of petroleum were known.

Growth of the industry was also impeded by its production methods. All over Europe the seepages were worked with hand-shafts, sometimes shallow holes, sometimes deeper shafts sunk to a maximum depth of 200 feet and properly timbered by specialists, hired for the purpose by the farmers or landowners. However, there was no well-planned production from a larger area. Landowners and farmers produced from small plots and sold their oil on the local market to tradesmen and pedlars, who sometimes delivered their oil to refiners. Thus in Galicia we find no less than 151 villages involved, in 1860, in the production of oil from hundreds of shafts, a primitive method stimulated by the high price of the oil. In the decade following Drake's discovery, Galician oil fetched $140 — per ton! Such primitive production methods had been in use in Galicia from the seventeenth century onwards, and in Roumania even a century earlier. Neither landowners nor farmers were prepared to spend capital in drilling for oil. This is remarkable if we remember that drilling methods had been developed in Europe from the middle of the eighteenth century and stimulated by the reports of missionaries on the ancient Chinese drilling methods. These new tools and methods were used extensively in the drilling for water, coal, and salt, they had been adopted in the United States, and they had even been used locally to drill for oil. Thus Professor Hunäus of Hannover sank ten wells near Wietze, between the years 1857 and 1863, for the specific purpose of finding oil, but only three of them showed traces of oil. These European drilling methods, after traveling to the New World and being adapted to oil, were to travel back to their home country to be applied around 1880 in Galicia and Roumania.

This lack of capital and of concentrated efforts also played its part in yet another factor retarding developments of the oil industry in Eastern Europe: transport. Whereas Western Europe has a well-developed highway and canal system, this was hardly true of Austria-Hungary and Roumania about 1850. Thus Joseph Hecker, who had produced good lamp oil from the crude of shafts near Boryslaw in 1810, had succeeded in supplying the nearby town of Drohobycz, but he failed to establish regular supplies to the more important markets in his native town Prague and in 1817 he had to give up. By 1852, when Lukasiewicz rediscovered the process of distilling and refining a good kerosene from Galician crude, the situation had changed. Jewish and Austrian bankers were now gradually supplying sufficient capital for more concentrated efforts. Lukasiewicz therefore not only established a stable supply to his customers in Lwow and other Galician towns, but also was in 1859 supplying the State Railways at Vienna with a 55-ton consignment.

Roumania was more favourably situated than Galicia from the point of view of transport. At the turn of the eighteenth century some 20 tons a year were produced from handshafts, but this production rose rapidly when, in the 1840's, the prince Bibesco tried to interest two Russian bankers in the production of petroleum on his lands. Though this attempt failed, others profited from the fact that the petroleum and its products could be transported by carts a distance of some 10 to 15 miles to the river Danube (and later to the railways) to be shipped upstream to the important markets in Austria and beyond. This market helped the rise of petroleum production in Roumania for, in many years, imports of American petroleum products were restricted by a heavy tariff to which the Roumanian oil was not subjected.

Where Nature provided better transport facilities, industrial efforts to produce petroleum came fairly early. The first Roumanian refinery was built by N. Choss at Lucacesti in 1840. At the time Drake sank his well there were three refineries working in Roumania with a total capacity of some 4,000 tons a year, supplying lamp oil to Bucharest, the first city to be completely illuminated with kerosene lamps in 1859. By Drake's time Roumanian kerosene was sold as far as Vienna and Odessa. Curiously enough, the latter town used Roumanian oil rather than Russian oil from Baku, a center where handshafts had been working for centuries! However, transport difficulties between Baku and Odessa were such before the advent of the Baku-Batum pipeline (at the turn of the nineteenth century) that the cost of petroleum products rose a hundredfold! The market for the rich Caucasian oilfields remained the interior of Russia, which could be reached by shipping up the Volga River, rather than the Mediterranean countries. Here in Baku the first refinery was not opened by Mirzoeff until 1863.

Notwithstanding unplanned production, refining difficulties, and lack of transport facilities, the European petroleum industry managed to survive and develop against heavy competition. This circumstance was due to the fact that the industry applied all its ingenuity to the complete utilization of all petroleum fractions beyond the readily salable lamp oil. In 1831 Dolfuss had invented the viscometer. Before 1859, further studies of bearings and other applications of lubricants had paved the way for the manufacture of petroleum lubricants from Galician and Roumanian crude, though much remained to be done in this field. The production of paraffin wax, moreover, had become one of the main props of the oil industry of Eastern Europe. In 1830 Reichenback had discovered these white flaxes in wood-tar distillates. Later they were found in coal oil, shale oil, and certain crudes like the "Rangoon tar" from Burma. In the meantime the manufacture of good candles had profited from the introduction of impregnated woven wicks, casting machinery, and the manufacture of stearine from fats. The London firm of Price, founded in 1830, started marketing stearine candles in 1835 and switched over to paraffin wax candles in 1855, when Young was producing wax from his Scottish Boghead Coal at Bathgate. By 1857 Warren de la Rue had invented methods for producing good paraffin wax from the "Rangoon tar," imported in "metal tanks" from Burma.

In the 1850's the Galician refiners were starting to perfect the methods of producing paraffin wax, and they also attempted to refine the crude "mountain wax" or ceresine, which they mined locally in veins. The difficult separation of oily parts from the solid wax was not properly solved until the introduction of the sweating process in 1871, but the efforts of the Galician wax manufacturers were such that their machinery was adopted everywhere in the early days, and for the decades to come they were to be the teachers of the wax refineries to be erected in other parts of the world such as Burma and the East Indies.

In the same way, the light fractions of the Galician and Roumanian crudes were distilled and refined to be sold as paint thinners and solvents for the extraction of oil seeks, and so forth. The residue had been sold locally as fuel oil ever since the industry was established in these parts, but the honor of having discovered suitable oil burners goes to the Russians, whose "Astrakan burner" was used for heating houses with oil fuel before 1860. The Russians and French were the first to adapt the oil burner to shipping and railways, but this was not before the 1870's. The crude oil residue was sometimes turned into asphaltic bitumen, though the bitumen industry still relied heavily on the natural bitumens of Neufchatel, Val de Travers of Seyssel, in the Alps.

Little has appeared about this early European petroleum industry in most of our history books, probably because most of the evidence is buried in publications written in Roumanian or Polish. However, from the evidence available up to now it is perfectly clear that the industry not only managed to survive but actually developed in the face of heavy competition. Wholesale utilization and refining of all the fractions contained in the crudes not only made this possible but also laid the foundations of many techniques still common in the oil industry.

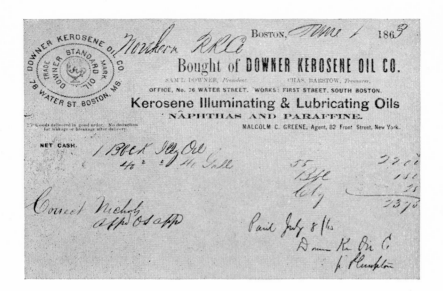

Founders' Incentives:
The Pre-Drake Refining Industry

by Kendall Beaton

SHELL OIL COMPANY

In their new book, *The American Petroleum Industry: The Age of Illumination,* Drs. Williamson and Daum point up the tremendous ferment in the field of lighting during the 30 years preceding the outbreak of the Civil War.[1] This was the period that saw the development of gas lighting and the introduction of a host of new substitute oils which their innovators hoped would be better and cheaper than whale oil, the quality illuminant ever since the late Middle Ages. This ferment of activity in illumination from 1830 onwards set the stage for the emergence of coal-oil illuminants in the 1850's.

[1] Harold F. Williamson and Arnold R. Daum, *The American Petroleum Industry: The Age of Illumination, 1859–1899* (Evanston, Ill., 1959), pp. 27–60.

This paper will examine some of the highlights of the coal-oil industry, for the markets it created and the refining methods it evolved were the incentives to innovation that impelled the founders of the modern petroleum industry — Drake and his backers — and made possible a ready sale for the crude oil from the new oil regions of western Pennsylvania.

Some idea of the size and substance of the coal-oil trade may be had from a survey made late in 1859 when the Drake well was only four months old. *Hunt's Merchants' Magazine* listed 34 coal-oil refineries, from St. Louis to Portland, with a total estimated output of some 22,750 gallons daily — between 500 and 600 barrels. At least $8,000,000 was invested in the coal-oil works, the magazine estimated, and they daily used 60,000 bushels of cannel coal, $2,000 worth of chemicals, and $1,000 worth of barrels. Value of the oil produced was placed at more than $5,000,000 per year, or $16,000 a day, indicating an average wholesale price at the refinery of about 70 cents a gallon. The number of workmen employed in these coal-oil works was put at 2,000; the number of miners required to produce cannel coal, 700; and the number of coopers to turn out barrels, 400 — a total payroll of 3,100 men directly. dependent upon the new industry, not to mention those engaged in the manufacture of treating chemicals or of lamps to burn the oil. The new industry was the more remarkable in that it had developed within five years and "two years ago, there were only two or three oil-works in the country." [2]

Of chief importance in the development of the new coal-oil business were the efforts of three groups of men: Dr. Abraham Gesner of Nova Scotia, who gave us the name *kerosene*, and who, with associates, set in motion the pioneer New York Kerosene Oil Works, the largest of the 1859 coal-oil plants; James Young, father of the Scottish shale-oil industry, a business which has persisted to this day; and Samuel Downer, Jr., of Boston, an alert whale-oil merchant and manufacturer who had the good business judgment to employ able technologists and to move with the times, converting first from whale oil to coal-oil manufacture and becoming finally the largest of the early petroleum refiners.[3]

But before proceeding with their story, a word about the rapid changes in the illuminating oil trade from 1840 onwards. Whale

[2] *Hunt's Merchants' Magazine and Commercial Review* (*Journal of Mining, Manufacturers, and Art, 1860*), vol. 42, pp. 245–246.
[3] See Kendall Beaton, "Dr. Gesner's Kerosene: The Start of American Oil Refining," *Business History Review* (March, 1955), pp. 28–53, and "The High Cost of Whale Oil — and What It Led To," *World Petroleum* (June, 1959), Section I, pp. 62–67.

oil, the standard of excellence in illumination for more than 500 years, had never been a poor man's light. Successions of European whalers — Basque, Dutch, French, English, and Scandinavian — had killed off the whales in European waters. With the establishment of the British colonies in North America and the discovery of whales on this side of the Atlantic, the whaling trade shifted to the New World, where the same process of exhaustion of nearby waters was repeated off Long Island and Cape Cod. The whalers of New Bedford, Gloucester, Nantucket, New London, Stonington, and Sag Harbor undertook progressively longer voyages — to the South Atlantic, then around Cape Horn and into the farthest reaches of the Pacific, running up their costs and the price of whale oil and bringing on, by the 1830's and 1840's, what is nostalgically remembered as the Golden Age of Whaling. It was of course a "golden age" for the whalers, not their customers. By the early 1850's, when the American whaling fleet numbered more than 700 vessels, sperm oil was bringing between $2.00 and $2.50 a gallon with good prospects of going as high as $5.00.[4]

In the face of these rising prices, a number of new oils gained increasing market prominence from 1830 onwards. Rapeseed, or colza, oil, pressed from the seed of a cabbage-family plant, spread from Germany and the Low Countries. It was safe to burn and its light was as bright as sperm oil's. Its price by the 1850's was also comparable: about $2.00 a gallon.[5]

America, with its abundant pine forests, developed a variety of illuminants from turpentine. One of these was sylvic, or rosin, oil, the heavy end of the turpentine fraction, which produced a comparatively dim flame and in the 1850's sold for 50 cents a gallon.[6] The most successful of the wood oils was camphene, a purified oil of turpentine distilled over quicklime to free it from impurities. A prominent early camphene manufacturer was Isiah Jennings of New York, who took out a number of patents on turpentine distillation during the 1830's.[7] Camphene burned better than rosin oil, produced a bright flame, and was widely manufactured in the 1840's and 1850's, selling for about 65 cents a gallon.[8] Because of its low

---

[4] See L. Harrison Matthews, "A Note on Whaling," *A History of Technology* (Oxford, 1958), vol. IV, pp. 53–63; prices mentioned in Benjamin Silliman, Jr., *Report on the Rock Oil, or Petroleum, of Venango Co., Pennsylvania* (New Haven, 1855), p. 19; and Joshua Merrill reminiscences, *The Derrick's Hand-Book of Petroleum* (Oil City, Pa., 1898), p. 889.
[5] Price from Silliman report, p. 19.
[6] *Ibid.*; definition of rosin oil from *Century Dictionary*, 1889.
[7] Composition of camphene, *Century Dictionary*, 1889; F. W. Robins, *The Story of the Lamp (and the Candle)*, (London, 1939), p. 110; Jennings patents of Oct. 10, 1830, June 13, 1831, Aug. 27, 1835, July 1, 1836, July 23, 1836, and Dec. 31, 1839.
[8] Prices from Silliman report, p. 19, and circular in Landauer Collection, New-York Historical Society, "Kerosene Oils, Distilled from Coal" (New York, 1857), p. 2.

boiling and ignition points, camphene was highly inflammable and a dangerous fuel; its burning properties could be improved by mixing it with two to three parts of alcohol. This mixture, generally called "burning fluid," or sometimes simply "camphene," tended to vaporize rapidly, giving it a disturbing tendency to explode. Another substitute oil developed and widely sold in America in the years following 1835 was lard oil. Lard oil was a safe, but dim, light and cost more than a dollar a gallon.

None of these substitutes for whale oil was really satisfactory. Colza oil cost almost as much as the genuine article; rosin oil, the cheapest, was a poor illuminant; lard was safe, dim, and fairly expensive; camphene and burning fluid, while extremely dangerous to use, gave off a good light for relatively little money. They were in consequence the most widely sold of the "artificial illuminants."

There was plenty of room for successors to these substitutes. Many who left little record of their attempts tried and failed to produce oils that would be brighter, cheaper, or less dangerous to use. A chief obstacle to most of these would-be innovators was that they were "practical" men with little knowledge of chemistry, a bad handicap, for "artificial" oils had to be "rectified" or "refined" chemically to remove impurities that caused bad burning and foul odors. When truly successful substitutes at last appeared just before the Civil War, they were the work of men with a good knowledge of chemistry.

Of prime importance in the establishment of the "coal-oil" business was Dr. Abraham Gesner (1797–1864), Canadian physician, geologist, author, and inveterate experimenter. As an outgrowth of his geological interests, Gesner had, early in 1846, demonstrated at public lectures on Prince Edward Island a lamp oil which he had distilled from asphalt from the Great Pitch Lake of Trinidad.[9] In 1849, Gesner discovered in Albert County, New Brunswick, a vein of bituminous rock called "Albert coal," and today known as albertite. He turned his hand to this nearby material and distilled a lamp oil from it. During the next few years he made several trips to New York in attempts to interest gas manufacturers in Albert coal as a raw material.[10] No direct evidence exists on the success of these efforts, but we do know that by 1857, at least, the Boston Gas Light Company was using Albert coal for gas enrichment.[11]

[9] Abraham Gesner, M.D., *A Practical Treatise on Coal, Petroleum, and Other Distilled Oils* (New York, 1861), pp. 8-9.
[10] Williamson and Daum, *Age of Illumination*, p. 45.
[11] Merrill reminiscences, p. 883.

In the spring of 1853, Gesner, in his fifty-sixth year, moved to New York, applied for American patents on his process for making illuminating oil from bituminous materials, and set about enlisting capital to engage in the manufacture of kerosene, a trade name he had coined from the Greek *keros*, meaning *wax*, and the *-ene* ending of camphene, then the most widely sold of the artificial illuminants.[12] An eight-page prospectus issued at New York in March, 1853, called for formation of a joint stock company of $100,000 capital to manufacture a complete range of products from kerosene to asphalt, including besides kerosene, naphthas for paint and rubber manufacture, railway grease, mineral pitch for varnish, "hydraulic concrete" for waterproofing and paving, paraffin for candles, coke and gas for burning "in the manufactory," and ammonia ash for fertilizer.[13]

This projection of the products that could be made by an oil refinery is ample evidence of Gesner's technological soundness and business foresight. It preceded by two full years the much more famous report of Prof. Benjamin Silliman, Jr., of Yale, who also accurately forecast many of the useful products that would be made from petroleum in the years to come. Gesner's list of products is longer than Silliman's and each of the nine products he forecast was eventually manufactured by the petroleum industry, although in many cases only after decades of foot-dragging on the part of the "practical" refiners who dominated the refining scene for a full half century.

Gesner obviously believed that kerosene illuminating oil was the product of most immediate promise for the new enterprise. His patents, issued in June, 1854, were three in number and covered the process of distilling and treating three separate kerosenes from "bitumen wherever found." [14] Meanwhile, the projected corporation had been organized early in 1854 by a group of New York businessmen under the name North American Kerosene Gas Light Company and seven acres along Newtown Creek in Queens purchased for a plant site. Following custom of the day, the Kerosene Works chose not to handle its own sales but appointed sales agents for the task, the brothers John H. and George W. Austen, sons of a prominent New York merchant. The Austens opened sales offices at 50 Beaver

[12] *Engineering and Mining Journal* (Feb. 9, 1884), p. 99; account is unsigned but the author was probably George Weldten Gesner, son of Dr. Gesner.
[13] Circular in Landauer Collection, New-York Historical Society, "Project for the Formation of a Company to Work Under the Combined Patent Rights (for the State of New York) of Dr. Abraham Gesner, of Halifax, N.S., and the Rt. Hon. The Earl of Dundonald, of Middlesex, England" (New York; March, 1853).
[14] U.S. Patent Nos. 11,203, 11,204, 11,205 (June 27, 1854).

Street, New York, and began a vigorous campaign to introduce the new illuminant, along with a suitable lamp for burning it. Kerosene burned well in the expensive Argand lamp used for sperm oil, but John Austen sought a cheaper lamp. He found an inexpensive flat-wick metal lamp with glass chimney in Vienna. This so-called "Vienna burner" was widely copied and became the model for our common kerosene lamp.[15]

This little incident of Austen's finding in Vienna a lamp eminently suited to kerosene has long served as a warning to many doing oil history research that the full story of early kerosene refining is missing many important particulars — a lack that Professor Forbes has now supplied.[16]

The Kerosene Works on Newtown Creek got into operation some time in 1854.[17] "The new illuminating oil," Dr. Gesner's son wrote some years later, "met with strongest opposition from the turpentine and alcohol trades." [18] However, the relative safety, superior light, and reasonable prices of kerosene gave its manufacturers sales arguments that were hard to put down. A circular issued by the Austens in 1857 is replete with laboratory tests comparing the main illuminants then on the market. In intensity of light, kerosene outshone its competitors by a wide margin. Kerosene was then selling for $1.00 a gallon, as against $2.25 for sperm oil, $1.50 for colza oil, $1.25 for lard oil, 87 cents for burning fluid, 63 cents for camphene, and 50 cents a gallon for rosin oil. The brilliance of kerosene and its economy of combustion gave it impressive advantages when reduced to "cost of an equal amount of light." On this basis, burning fluid was seven times as costly as kerosene, sperm oil six times as expensive, and so on down the scale.[19]

As kerosene's acceptance spread, the Kerosene Works on Newtown Creek expanded. A lengthy description of the bustling plant was printed in the New York *Commercial Advertiser* in August, 1859, just three days before the completion of the Drake well. Its output was then running at the rate of 5,000 gallons a day; raw material, by this time Boghead coal from Scotland, was being imported at the rate of 30,000 tons a year; the plant had its own

[15] Merrill reminiscences.
[16] R. J. Forbes, *More Studies in Early Petroleum History* (Leiden, Netherlands, 1959), pp. 91–107.
[17] Abraham Gesner, M.D., *A Practical Treatise on Coal, Petroleum, and Other Distilled Oils*, 2d ed. (New York, 1865), revised by George Weldten Gesner, p. 10; and New York *Commercial Advertiser* (Aug. 24, 1859), give starting date as 1854; earliest business record that has come to light is invoice from Austens, Agents for North American Kerosene Gas Light Co., dated Nov. 16, 1855, in private collection of I. Warshaw, New York.
[18] *Engineering and Mining Journal* (see note 12).
[19] Circular "Kerosene Oils, Distilled From Coals," 1857, in Landauer Collection, New-York Historical Society.

cooperage, employed 200 regular hands, and had another 25 men who "find constant employment in erecting buildings and putting up machinery." In addition to kerosene, the Kerosene Works was making binnacle oil for ships, solid paraffin for candles, a naphtha called "Kerosoline" for cleaning silk and wool, and lubricating oil for machinery.[20] The main product, kerosene, was then selling for $1.15 a gallon at the refinery; a report made a few months later shows the company's costs as 63 cents a gallon.[21] With such handsome profits to be made, it is no wonder that formidable competitors were appearing on the scene — although the New York Kerosene Oil Company, as it was now called, remained the largest.

The competitors of greatest interest and importance were James Young of Bathgate, Scotland, and Samuel Downer, Jr., of South Boston. Both enterprises had initially entered the coal-oil business as producers of "artificial" lubricants to replace the animal and vegetable oils then on the market.

James Young (1811–1883) deservedly gets the credit for establishing the Scottish shale-oil industry; he is also frequently credited with instituting the first manufacture of coal-oil illuminants. While he cannot be accorded this honor, which properly belongs to Dr. Gesner, Young's technical achievements were nevertheless of first magnitude. He also had the advantage of having preceded Gesner to the patent office.

A Glasgow-born, college-trained chemist, Young was managing an alkali works at Manchester in 1847, when the owner of a Derbyshire coal mine approached him with a problem. The mine had developed a petroleum seepage which produced some 300 gallons a day of a thick, black crude oil. It was a safety hazard and disposal nuisance. Could Mr. Young make something useful out of it? Young reported that lubricating oils and paraffin could be made from the crude oil, and late in 1848 formed a partnership with the mine owner to exploit this small crude oil production.[22]

Young soon realized that 300 gallons daily was too small a supply for a successful commercial enterprise. He reasoned, although incorrectly, that the crude oil found in the mine had been generated from coal by subterranean heat and set about reproducing this reaction in his laboratory. "I started an investigation," Young later wrote, "with the prospect of procuring petroleum, or a substance equivalent to it, from coal and after some time succeeded. . . .

[20] New York *Commercial Advertiser*, Aug. 24, 1859.
[21] Gesner, *Practical Treatise* (1861), p. 21.
[22] Edwin M. Bailey, "James Young — Founder of the Mineral Oil Industry," *Institute of Petroleum Review* (London, 1948), vol. II, pp. 180–183, 216–221, 249–252; "The Dawn of Petroleum Refining," vol. II, pp. 357–360.

The process consists in the distillation of coal at the lowest possible temperature at which it can be decomposed. By this process we obtain a mixture of several liquids with paraffin dissolved in them. This liquid I named paraffin oil." [23] His method of distilling the bituminous coal for its paraffin content, treating the extract, and purifying the solid paraffin wax were described in a British patent of October 17, 1850, and a U.S. patent of March 23, 1852.

Cancelling his contract with the Derbyshire mine owner, Young moved to Bathgate, West Lothian, Scotland, in 1850–1851 and erected a new plant to work the nearby mineral deposits. He had as partners in this venture Edward Meldrum, a chemist formerly in his employ, and E. W. Binney, a Manchester lawyer and geologist. [24]

Although the products of Young's new plant and Gesner's Kerosene Works in New York were given the generic name "coal oil," the raw material was not in either case a true coal. Both the Albert mineral of New Brunswick, now called albertite, and the Torbane Hill mineral of Bathgate, later called torbanite, received the designation "coal" as a result of lawsuits involving mining rights. The validity of mining leases hinged upon whether or not the substance in question was coal. In both cases, the courts upheld the litigants claiming coal-mining privileges. Gesner sought to prove the asphaltic nature of the mineral and lost. [25] Young supported the other side of the argument, for his patents covered only the distillation of coal and would otherwise have been valueless. [26] It was, thus, a legal rather than a geological decision that made the new product "coal oil."

Young has often been erroneously credited with being the first to manufacture coal-oil illuminants. That this was not so we may gain from his own words. Writing of the event some time later he said that he and his partners "at first manufactured naphtha and lubricating oil. Paraffin oil for burning and solid paraffin were not sold until 1856, and the demand for it only became considerable in 1859." [27]

This account ties in well with the recollections of Joshua Merrill, for many years superintendent of the Downer Works at South Boston. Samuel Downer, Jr. (1807–1881) was a prosperous whale-

[23] Bailey, "Dawn of Petroleum Refining," p. 359.
[24] *Ibid.*, and "James Young," p. 218.
[25] "Report of a Case Tried at Albert Circuit, 1852, by His Honor Judge Wilmot and a Special Jury. *Abraham Gesner* vs. *William Cairns*," Saint John, N.B., 1853.
[26] H. R. J. Conacher, "History of the Scottish Oil-Shale Industry," *The Oil-shales of the Lothians*, 3d ed. (London, 1927), p. 245. Style of the case was *Gillespie* v. *Russell*, Court of Session (Scotland), 1854–1856–1857.
[27] Bailey, "Dawn of Petroleum Refining," p. 359. Bailey had access to Young's diaries, notebooks and correspondence; he does not identify the source of this particular quotation.

oil merchant and had manufactured sperm candles since 1834. Looking for a lubricating oil which would perform better than whale oil in high-speed machinery, Downer bought a struggling firm at Waltham known as the United States Chemical Manufacturing Company. This enterprise had been organized by Dr. Samuel R. Philbrick and the brothers Luther and William Atwood to make and market a lubricating oil from by-product coal tar. Dr. Philbrick and the Atwoods were competent technical men, but they had great difficulty in overcoming the strong odor of their coal-tar lubricating oil. Merrill, who was their salesman at the time, reported that 90 per cent of their customers could not be induced to place a second order. Downer seemed on the verge of losing his investment when, in 1855, a letter arrived from Scotland that changed the course of events.[28]

George Miller & Co., manufacturers of coal-tar naphthas in Glasgow, had heard of the process to distill lubricating oil from coal tar and wanted to install it. Luther Atwood had developed the process and held the patent, so Downer dispatched him to Glasgow and there Atwood remained a year building and installing the manufacturing apparatus. The Crimean War was then in progress and naphthas were much in demand for solvents in the manufacture of mackintosh rubber goods. To supplement their own naphtha production, the Miller firm bought from other manufacturers, including Young's works at Bathgate. Luther Atwood, always the experimenter, took some of this naphtha from Young's plant and by treatment made it into a water-white illuminating oil.

This oil was burning in a lamp in the Miller offices one day in 1856 when Young dropped in. Miller told him, "That is some of your brown Bathgate naphtha that our chemist has been manipulating and refining, and there is a sample of the oil." [29] Young promptly stopped selling his naphtha to others, and began manufacture of an illuminating oil which he called "paraffin oil." Most of the initial shipments of his new illuminant went to Austria, where a hydrocarbon oil trade already existed, but in a few years, Young's lamp oil was in use throughout the British Isles, where the name he gave it, *paraffin*, is still the term in common use.

In the fall of 1856, Luther Atwood and Merrill, who had also been in Glasgow part of the time, returned to Boston full of enthusiasm for the manufacture of a similar lamp oil. Against Downer's better judgment (he was, after all, still in the whale-oil

[28] This and following paragraph from Merrill reminiscences, *Derrick's Hand-Book*.
[29] Merrill reminiscences, p. 881.

business and had just poured several thousands of dollars into facilities to make coal-tar lubricating oil), the Atwood brothers and Merrill set about distilling lamp oil from Trinidad asphalt, and experienced encouraging local sales.[30] By early 1857, Downer was completely won over. He sold his whale-oil business to two former employees, contracted for steady supplies of Albert coal from New Brunswick, and began building coal-oil works in earnest.[31] By the fall of 1858, he had $150,000 invested in new plant, 50 retorts operating around the clock, and an unsold inventory of 200,000 gallons. He was beginning to doubt the wisdom of his boldness when the new product caught on. During that fall and winter of 1858–1859 the accumulated inventory was sold and demand even got ahead of production. With prices of $1.35 to $1.40 a gallon at the refinery, Downer had by spring cleared more than $100,000. He promptly built a second plant at Portland, putting Dr. Philbrick and William Atwood in charge.[32]

Luther Atwood had meanwhile become chief chemist of the Kerosene Works on Newtown Creek. Through this friendly connection, Downer early in 1859 licensed the right to use the name "Kerosene," then still a patent trade name, and changed the names of his Boston and Portland companies to embody the Kerosene name.[33]

As protection of the Kerosene refining process, the Gesner patents were not so successful. Young's British patent of 1850 and U.S. patent of 1852 had precedence over Gesner's 1854 patents. Soon after he began manufacture of lamp oil in 1856, Young turned to his American competitors and, by threat of infringement suits, convinced many of them, including Downer and the New York Kerosene Works, to become licensees at a royalty of 2 cents a gallon.[34]

Gesner's chief connection with the New York Kerosene Works had been through his patents; when this company became a licensee of Young, Gesner's influence in the firm's affairs went into eclipse. He continued the practice of medicine, taking time out to assist his sons who, as consulting chemists, were frequently engaged to design and set up some of the newer coal-oil works that were being established near cannel-coal deposits in West Virginia, Ohio,

---

[30] *Ibid.*
[31] Billheads in collection of I. Warshaw, New York.
[32] Merrill reminiscences.
[33] Circular letters from New York Kerosene Oil Company, Boston Kerosene Oil Company, and Portland Kerosene Oil Company, March 28, 1859, in Landauer Collection, New-York Historical Society.
[34] Bailey, "James Young," p. 180.

and Kentucky. In 1860, Gesner compiled an authoritative handbook for illuminating oil refiners and it was published early in 1861. For many years thereafter Gesner's *Practical Treatise on Coal, Petroleum, and Other Distilled Oils* was the standard work in its field. Two years later, Dr. Gesner returned to his native Nova Scotia, and was about to become professor of natural history at Dalhousie when he died early in 1864.

Although he clearly deserves a large measure of credit for the establishment of the coal-oil industry, circumstances conspired to keep Gesner from fame and fortune in the business he started. Unlike Young and Downer, Gesner had no large proprietary interest in the business; again, unlike Young and Downer, he had age against him, being in his fifty-eighth year when the Kerosene Works started operation; he continued in a profession rather than embarking upon a business career; and lastly, Gesner's well-drawn and well-conceived patents were made valueless by legal decisions that bituminous rock was "coal." In the face of such handicaps to fame, it is not surprising that Gesner's role as a pioneer is only now being fully appreciated.

The completion of the Drake well brought crisis to the new coal-oil industry. But it was already in trouble before this historic event. The editor of *Hunt's Merchants' Magazine*, commenting upon his survey of the coal-oil industry at the close of 1859, pointed to a complaint that has haunted oil refining ever since: too many people making too much product. Production of lamp oil at the end of 1859, he calculated, was running more than 10 per cent ahead of consumption. The first casualty to economics was the pioneer New York Kerosene Works. It went into bankruptcy in the spring of 1860 and its works, which had cost $450,000 to build, were auctioned off to Peter Cooper, Jr., W. H. Appleton (head of the famous publishing house), and Abraham M. Cozzens for $96,-000. The company had made a profit of $120,000 in five years of business but "by overtrading and various misfortunes lost on the works, coal, etc., at least $300,000." [35] Under the management of Cozzens & Co., the plant on Newtown Creek converted to petroleum; and by the late 1860's, it had become the Queens County Oil Works, R. W. Burke, Agent; and in 1876, it passed into the hands of Chas. Pratt & Co., part of the growing Standard Oil Company. [36]

[35] *American Gas-Light Journal*, vol. I (June 1, 1860), p. 250.
[36] As the Queens Works of Standard Oil Co. of New York (later Socony-Vacuum Oil Co.), the old Kerosene Works operated as a lubricating oil plant until May, 1951. See Kendall Beaton, *Business History Review*, vol. XXIX (March, 1955), p. 53.

Downer, as soon as he could be sure that petroleum was the coming thing, moved with characteristic vigor. Late in 1861, he built the largest and most complete of the early Oil Region refineries at Corry, Pennsylvania. Under the trade-mark "Downer's Standard Oil," his product was energetically marketed at home and abroad, the first of the American brands to have extensive acceptance outside the United States. His trade name proved prophetic, for his companies, too, eventually passed into the hands of Standard Oil.

Young, who allowed that the new petroleum business "is ephemeral and won't last," continued on in the shale-oil business.[37] When his patents expired in 1864, he organized a joint-stock company, Young's Paraffin Light & Mineral Oil Co., Ltd., which stayed in the forefront of the Scottish shale-oil industry, a business which managed to survive the years by careful attention to by-products such as ammonium sulphate. Young's company lives on today as a subsidiary of the British Petroleum Company, Ltd.

During the first year of the new petroleum industry, the price of crude oil remained high. Oil produced in 1859 brought $20 a barrel, and prices in 1860 ran from $16 down to $8.80, with the average for the year reported at $9.60 a barrel.[38] Even at these high prices, petroleum was an attractive raw material for lamp-oil manufacture, for, being liquid, it eliminated the most costly part of coal-oil manufacture: the destructive distillation of solid material. This destructive distillation was expensive in terms of fuel consumption, and the retorts for the purpose represented the largest part of a coal-oil refiner's capital investment. By November, 1860, 15 new refineries had been built to work petroleum exclusively.[39]

Then came 1861, which was the "moment of truth" for coal-oil refiners. That year the price of crude oil, as the result of large production, dropped to an average of 52 cents a barrel. Most of the coal-oil refiners who had chosen backwoods locations in order to be near cannel-coal seams calculated their economics and quietly went out of business. Others, located near metropolitan markets, converted to petroleum and became factors in the new petroleum refining business.

And so ended the brief but important history of American coal oil. In five years, these lamp oils revolutionized illumination, introduced cheap lamps and inexpensive burning oils to the average home,

[37] Merrill reminiscences, p. 882.
[38] Prices from Thomas A. Gale, *The Wonder of the Nineteenth Century: Rock Oil in Pennsylvania and Elsewhere* (Erie, Pennsylvania, 1860), p. 33; *The Petroleum Almanac* (New York, 1946), p. 37a.
[39] Gesner, *Practical Treatise* (1861), pp. 128–129.

and provided the markets and refining methods on which the American petroleum industry would be built. Although the coal-oil industry's life was short, it was a highly useful one and illustrated, in the words of a contemporary editor, "the impetuous energy with which the American mind takes up any branch of industry that promises to pay well." [40]

[40] *Hunt's Merchants' Magazine and Commercial Review* (*Journal of Mining, Manufacturers, and Art*), vol. 42 (1860), p. 246.

The Significance
of the Drake Well

by Paul H. Giddens

HAMLINE UNIVERSITY

Seminars are not unique, but the Centennial Seminar on the History of the Petroleum Industry is unique for several reasons: it is devoted exclusively to a study of the petroleum industry; it is composed of professionally trained persons — historians, economists, lawyers, and others; and it is the first of its kind to be held. Considering the profound effect that the petroleum industry has had upon society at home and abroad during the last one hundred years, the holding of this Centennial Seminar is most appropriate. I congratulate the Harvard Graduate School of Business Administration and those responsible for the seminar for planning such a significant event during the Centennial year.

Twenty-five years ago, when I started my research and writing on the petroleum industry, it would have been very difficult to have organized such a specialized seminar. At that time, there was little interest in oil history on the part of either scholars, oilmen, or the industry. I recall making a survey, in 1934, of the literature on the historical and economic aspects of the development of the petroleum industry. There were scarcely any professionally trained scholars doing research and writing in the field. Although there were some books on technical and legal aspects of the industry, scholars had paid little attention to its historical and economic aspects.

As I look about the room this morning, note the number of persons who have been active in research and writing on the petroleum industry, and think of the growing list of scholarly books published about the industry within the past twenty years, it is clear just how remarkable a change has taken place since 1934. The holding of this Centennial Seminar is proof of the change. From the point of view of a veteran who has been doing research and writing on the petroleum industry for twenty-five years, I am more than pleased to note the growth of scholarly activity and the development of this interest in its history.

Much of the background leading to the drilling of the Drake well has already been presented this morning by my good friends, R. J. Forbes and Kendall Beaton. They have paved the way for me in excellent fashion.

In order to understand the significance of the Drake well, it is necessary at the outset to dispose of some familiar myths. In the first place, it should be abundantly clear that in drilling for oil Colonel E. L. Drake did not discover petroleum. Professor Forbes in his talk and in his writings has emphasized that a knowledge of and the use of petroleum goes far back into ancient times.[1] In our own country, petroleum was known to exist as early as 1627.[2] Lewis Evans indicated the presence of petroleum on his map of the Middle Colonies published in 1755. Travelers and soldiers during the eighteenth and early nineteenth centuries noted the existence of oil springs in western New York, western Pennsylvania, West Virginia, and Ohio.

The second myth to be demolished is that the Drake well was the first to produce petroleum in the United States. Many salt wells in western Pennsylvania, West Virginia, Kentucky, and Ohio produced petroleum long before the drilling of the Drake

[1] R. J. Forbes, *Studies in Early Petroleum History* (Leiden, 1958); *More Studies in Early Petroleum History, 1860–1880* (Leiden, 1959).
[2] Paul H. Giddens, *The Birth of the Oil Industry* (New York, 1938), chap. 1.

well in 1859. The oil was either dumped or was marketed in very limited quantities, principally as medicine. But the production of petroleum was *accidental* and *incidental*, rather than the result of a deliberate effort to obtain petroleum.

Much publicity has been given to the Williams well in Canada as being the first oil well in North America.[3] In view of the previously mentioned production of oil in salt wells, it is difficult to substantiate the claims for the Williams well. Whether it antedated the Drake well has not been established. Even if it did, the Williams well would not adversely affect the historic place of the Drake well because the Canadian well was *dug*, not drilled. More important is the fact that even after the Williams well was completed nothing happened. It was a single, isolated event without any subsequent effects.

If Drake did not discover petroleum and was not the first to produce petroleum in the United States, what then is the significance of the Drake well?[4] I could be brief and say that in a sense everything the petroleum industry is today is a result of the drilling of the Drake well. However, I wish to emphasize the immediate significance of this event.

The reason for organizing the Pennsylvania Rock Oil Company of New York, and later the Seneca Oil Company, and for sending Drake to Titusville in 1858 was *specifically* to obtain petroleum in large enough quantities so that it might be marketed commercially. Prior to the drilling of the Drake well, petroleum had been skimmed from oil springs and creeks or obtained by throwing a flannel or woolen blanket on top of the oil springs or creeks and letting it absorb the oil. In other instances it was produced incidentally in salt wells. These methods did not produce enough oil to market on an extensive scale. Therefore, the Drake well is significant because Drake was employed by the Seneca Oil Company and sent to Titusville for the *deliberate* purpose of obtaining petroleum in large commercial quantities. Drake's main objective was clear and his finding of oil in large quantities was not *incidental*.

Drake arrived in Titusville in the spring of 1858, began collecting oil from the springs on the Brewer, Watson & Company farm, started to dig a well, abandoned the idea because of water and cave-ins, and decided to drill for oil. Thus the Drake well

---

[3] Paul H. Giddens, "History Upholds Drake's Claim to Fame," *The Titusville Herald* (July 9, 1952); Ernest C. Miller, "North America's First Oil Well — Who Drilled It?" *The Western Pennsylvania Historical Magazine*, vol. XLII, No. 4 (Dec., 1959).
[4] Giddens, *The Birth of the Oil Industry*, chaps. 3 and 4.

is also significant because it was the first oil well to be deliberately drilled, not dug.

The drilling method Drake used became standard practice for years to come, but his contribution was in the application — not the technique — of drilling. There was little or no originality to this method; it had been used for years in producing salt. On his first trip to Titusville in December, 1857, Drake stopped to see some salt wells in operation in Syracuse, New York. He also observed the salt wells at Tarentum, Pennsylvania. Upon his return to Titusville in the spring of 1858, he again went to Tarentum to consult with salt well owners and to hire a salt well driller. It was with many of the techniques and tools employed in drilling for salt that Drake drilled his famous well.

While petroleum had been used as an illuminant and lubricant in a few localities prior to 1859, Drake's well demonstrated convincingly that large deposits of petroleum lay beneath the earth's surface. His discovery opened a vast source of petroleum at a critical time in world history and made possible the production and marketing of petroleum in commercial quantities. Mr. Beaton has already discussed the growing shortage of oil for illuminating and lubricating purposes and the efforts to overcome this shortage during the 1840's and 1850's. What Drake did at Titusville in 1859 was a link and, as it turned out, a most important one, in the search for a new and better source of raw materials. Kerosene from petroleum relieved the growing shortage of illuminating oil, supplanted costlier and dangerous illuminants, and provided consumers with a cheap, safe, and efficient illuminant. Petroleum also provided an abundance of lubricants which greatly facilitated the progress of the Industrial Revolution, already well on its way in 1859.

Finally, the Drake well, by helping to create a new industry on the eve of the outbreak of the Civil War, took on considerable political significance. This event was an unexpected but fortunate development for the Union. The petroleum industry provided a stimulus to many branches of business and industry and acted as a powerful force in strengthening the economy of the North in a time of national crisis.[5] Coopers worked to capacity. Rolling mills found a market for an immense amount of hoop iron. Tinners made 5-gallon and 10-gallon cans by the thousand. Chemical factories ran at capacity producing alkali and acid. Machinists had more orders for steam engines and boilers than they could supply. Glass manufacturers benefited from a booming business in lamps, globes, and

[5] *Ibid.*, chap. 15.

chimneys. Railroads were built into the oil region, and the oil traffic assumed enormous proportions.

The new industry was of major importance to the Union in other respects. Petroleum was used to treat the wounds of Union soldiers. It became a substitute for turpentine, which had come from the South. Under the laws of July 1, 1862, and of June 30, 1864, levying a federal tax on crude and refined oil, Union revenues were increased by more than $8,000,000. The federal government also obtained considerable internal revenue from a newly created occupational group — the oilmen — under the new income tax law. When the South seceded, the Union no longer could count cotton exports among its assets, and consequently began to experience an increasingly unfavorable balance of trade. The situation was further aggravated by a decline in the export of breadstuffs after 1863. With the birth and growth of the petroleum industry and the development of a large export trade in oil, the Union's unfavorable balance of trade was to a considerable extent offset. In 1866 *The New York World* pointed out that petroleum exports in 1866, valued at about $20,000,000, were nearly enough to pay the interest on the bonds of the United States held in Europe. Writing about the role of petroleum in the Civil War, Sir S. Morton Peto, a London banker, said that it was "difficult to find a parallel to such a blessing bestowed upon a nation in the hour of her direst necessity." [6]

Profound though the specific and immediate repercussions were, however, Drake's well has a larger place in history. Although a small producer, it created fierce excitement in and outside the oil region. Thousands of men rushed to Oil Creek to lease or buy land and drill for oil; hundreds of wells were soon being drilled. In short, the completion of the Drake well set in motion the forces that created the American Petroleum Industry.

[6] S. Morton Peto, *Resources and Prospects of America, Ascertained During a Visit to the States in the Autumn of 1865* (London, 1866), p. 206.

The Rise of Big Business in the Oil Industry

by Henrietta M. Larson

HARVARD BUSINESS SCHOOL

It is especially appropriate on this occasion to discuss the rise of big business because this form of organization first developed in America in the oil industry. A large, vertically integrated, centrally administered concern, operating world-wide, first appeared in the American oil industry in the decade of the 1870's and reached a high development in the next decade. In the 1880's this type began to spread in the industry, and within another score of years competition on this new level of organization was well established.

In discussing the rise of big business in the oil industry, attention must of necessity be focused on the Standard Oil group, the original leader in this development. It might appear that little that is new could be said about the early decades of Standard Oil; the concern has been the subject of more controversy and more historical writing than any other American business enterprise. Standard Oil's early years have lived on in history as an example of destructive, monopolistic exploitation — the name, indeed, has become a virtual folk symbol of monopoly.

However, books published in recent years, notably Allan Nevins' biography of John D. Rockefeller and Ralph W. and Muriel E. Hidy's *Pioneering in Big Business,* have provided a wealth of new information about the company's career and have afforded new insights into Standard Oil's rise and growth. Other recent studies — of other companies and of particular developments in the whole industry — have broadened our knowledge. Harold F. Williamson's and Arnold F. Daum's recently published history of the American oil industry to 1900 provides much new information and presents that history in broad perspective.

I

The historical significance of the rise within the oil industry of this new type of business concern can be envisioned only as it is compared with the general structure and functioning of the American business system at the time when the Standard Oil combination was in the process of formation. That system then functioned, as it had done from colonial days, in four types of markets: the local, regional, inter-regional or national, and international.

Within each of these markets, functional specialization was the rule. By far the most common figure was the businessman whom Professor N. S. B. Gras called the petty capitalist; the most dynamic was the larger-scale specialist whom Professor Gras called the industrial capitalist, operating as an individual or in a firm. This larger specialized businessman or unit had first appeared late in the eighteenth century and had risen in more and more industries as the Industrial Revolution advanced and transportation improved. Banks in urban centers, and manufacturers, railroads and steamship companies, wholesale distributors and exporters, all typically specialized in one industry, one function, or even one product or service. The transfer of goods and payments between regions and in foreign trade had come to be performed, principally, by public carriers, bankers, and wholesalers, instead of by the earlier merchants carrying on a large and diversified business.

These specialized entrepreneurs or enterprises were limited by their markets; probably few had reached their optimum size. The ownership organizations were mostly individual proprietorships or partnerships; however, railroads were incorporated, as were banks (other than the private banking concerns) and, increasingly, manufacturing concerns. There were no provisions in the general corporation statutes of the states for companies to own stock in other corporations, which lack, because of the power of states to determine the conditions under which foreign corporations could operate within their boundaries, placed a potential and often a real limitation on the extension of a corporation's business outside its home state. American corporation law was still based on a business system that was predominantly local or regional. Management of even the larger enterprises was commonly centered in one man, except in the case of railroads. Railroads had early acquired some professional management, but business units as a rule were run by owners or others who had risen from the ranks and whose experience and knowledge were narrowly limited.

This local or regional and generally simple system was probably the only economically feasible one so long as business was primarily on a regional basis and the inter-regional and international market for any one product was still thin. But the system proved too disjointed and uncoordinated to serve the larger demand that developed in certain fields in the second half of the nineteenth century with the westward extension of railroads and the lowering of transportation costs by land and sea, and with the increased industrialization and mechanization of production in the economy of the Western world. The larger volume of trade, particularly at first in certain consumer goods that increasingly found a market even in the lower reaches of the social structure with the wider distribution of purchasing power, stimulated businessmen to try new ways of reducing risks and increasing profits. Among these were efforts to increase volume and obtain control of related processes for purposes of defense or of profit.

The oil industry was the first in which the new type of business organization reached a high development. We may ask why this was so, and by what processes the large, vertically integrated concern grew. I shall attempt to present some answers to these questions, with respect not only to Standard Oil but also to the larger movement within the world oil industry which led to the establishment of competition on this new level of business organization. But first, let us look at the conditions in the American oil industry which made the rise of Standard Oil possible.

II

The oil industry in the early post-Civil War years was structured and managed like most other industries at the time. It was made up principally of small firms specializing in one function. Some, however, had grown to larger size and some had even begun to integrate backward and forward from their original operation. Outstanding in both the size of its operations and in its advances on the path of integration was Standard Oil of Ohio, incorporated in 1870. This company had developed from a small plant acquired in 1863 by John D. Rockefeller and a partner experienced in refining. The growth of Rockefeller's operations in Cleveland to 1870 foreshadowed the process by which the Standard Oil combination was to grow. From the very first, Rockefeller stressed the importance of large capacity and efficient operations as means of reducing costs and increasing profits. After the business in Cleveland became sufficiently large, Rockefeller reached out for greater control of raw materials costs and of the marketing of products by integrating backward and forward, including such auxiliary manufacturing operations as barrel making, and by achieving greater strength in bargaining for favorable transportation rates — as did other Cleveland refineries at the time. Rockefeller's operations grew by the addition of new partners and the expansion of refining. These partners added both capital assets and men of proved ability in the management of different oil industry operations. Rockefeller himself was, apparently, never primarily concerned with the management of operations but devoted himself largely to planning, policy formulation, and matters of strategy. By the time Standard Oil of Ohio had been created, he and his associates in the company were recognized as outstanding leaders by men who were making similar efforts to expand and strengthen their operations.

Conditions around 1870 were especially favorable to the rapid growth of the oil industry. Raw material was then available for expansion, the existing technology was adequate, and there was already a large — and potentially even a larger — domestic and foreign market for oil products. Proliferating industrial and transportation machines were requiring lubricants in increasing quantity and range of quality. But the great staple was kerosene, for which there was already a large market even at the currently high prices. The manufacture of kerosene in standard qualities was relatively simple; and this product, if handled with reasonable care, could without serious deterioration be stored for long periods and shipped any distance. There was every reason to believe that the oil industry faced a period of great expansion.

Certain developments early in the 1870's, however, introduced problems and uncertainties which upset the promise of a gradual evolution to serve an expanding market. One such development was a severe decline in product prices in 1871, which was followed by a downward trend of many years' duration. This price decline eventually affected the whole industry, but for several years it pressed hardest on refinery margins because refining capacity had been expanding faster than the supply of crude. Transportation was similarly affected because of its overcapacity relative to available traffic.

These developments, which appeared in most industries at the time, were especially disturbing to the oil industry because it was at best highly unstable. Its many small specialized firms had high unit costs and low profit margins which afforded little flexibility in time of trouble. The oil industry, moreover, was inherently unstable owing to the uncertainty of finding oil and the necessarily rapid development and early decline of pools under the American laws of ownership of oil and gas in the subsoil and the application of the common-law rule of capture to production from a reservoir. But because of the possibility of high profits, the oil-producing sector of the industry had attracted many inexperienced and adventuresome men with small capital. Both production and refining had a sizable percentage of marginal, and even submarginal, operators; the high rate of bankruptcy bespoke an unstable industry.

When trouble came in the form of price decline, the result was chaos. Everyone sought whatever shelter could be found. This situation was not unlike that then prevailing in the Minnesota wheat industry, where competing railroads, usually serving different regional sources of supply and markets and constituting segments of different routes to the consuming centers and ports in the East, sought traffic by giving special rates to those grain buyers or millers, or the two in combination, who gave promise of delivering the largest volume of traffic. In order to counter combinations of middlemen, processors, and transportation agencies, the farmers tried associations and political pressure without success. But no combination rose in the wheat industry comparable to Standard Oil in Pennsylvania's oil industry. This difference reflected, especially, differences in the geographical concentration of the two industries' raw materials at the time.

Like the various segments of the wheat industry, the oil producers, refiners, and carriers tried various ways to strengthen themselves, individually and collectively, when prices declined. Voluntary associations, pools, and political pressures were tried without success. Combinations proved the answer in the refining industry.

In 1874, under the pressure of price decline and after the failure of an association of refiners, the Standard Oil Alliance rose in refining under the leadership of Rockefeller and Standard Oil Company of Ohio. These allies moved aggressively in the direction of large-scale, vertically integrated operations. They first achieved dominant strength in refining, a strength based not only on size but also on efficient operations and favorable refinery locations. From the beginning they followed the policy of reaching backward and forward to obtain as large a measure of control of related operations as possible. By 1882 Standard Oil had gained unquestioned leadership in refining, in crude oil storage, and in the control of gathering lines in the Oil Regions; it had established auxiliary manufactures; it had built a trunkline to seaboard refineries; and it had entered extensively into wholesaling and jobbing.

Within the decade after 1882, the Standard Oil combination, then in a firmer union under the trust, continued to integrate horizontally and vertically. It entered strongly into production, in the Eastern oil regions but particularly in the new Lima-Indiana field; this expansion was undertaken principally to assure the combination of an adequate supply of raw materials to run pipelines and refineries to profitable capacity and of sufficient products for its markets. Entry into the Lima-Indiana field, however, promised to be profitable only if some process could be discovered for making marketable kerosene and other products from its highly sulphurous crude. Hence, Standard Oil turned successfully to chemical research, the first among the oil companies to do so. With large Midwestern production, it built a large new refinery at Whiting, Indiana. It also built pipelines from the Lima field to this new plant near Chicago and to its older refineries on the Eastern seaboard. It expanded its marketing in the Midwest and Far West. By the end of the decade Standard Oil's marketing extended throughout the United States, into Mexico and Canada, and to Europe and the distant reaches of the Orient. In brief, the Standard Oil Trust had built a large-volume, integrated, world-wide enterprise, which dominated the American and, indeed, the world oil industry.

It has been widely maintained that Rockefeller and his associates rose to dominance in the oil industry because of their monopolistic controls of strategically important factors, particularly of transportation. The knowledge we now have of the company's organization, administration, and operations indicates that their growth and strength rested on a broader base. They created a new type of organization which they expanded and administered so as to give them larger volume, more effective coordination of successive operations from the production of crude oil to the distribution of products, and better control of costs in nearly every operation. As has been noted, they first stabilized their refining by introducing efficient, large-scale operations and by locating their plants at strategically favorable points. They supported their refining combination by extending into related operations wherever possible as circumstances made such moves attractive for increasing earnings or necessary for defense. At the same time, they used their strategic locations and preponderent market and financial strength to gain every possible advantage, including competitively favorable transportation rates and dominance of pipeline transportation.

But, so runs this argument, their position and their strength rested primarily on their innovations in the structure, planning, and control of their enterprise which enabled them to operate successfully in a highly dynamic situation. These innovations, given the conditions under which the combination operated, enabled the Standard Oil group to attain great strength and to win over such other strong groups and vigorous competitors as the Tidewater Pipeline Company and the Pennsylvania Railroad and its allies.

III

The growth of Standard Oil through a process of cooperative combinations (that is, the union of many successful firms) shaped the essential features of the Standard Oil system for administering a large number of diverse, widely scattered, and changing operations. These were central planning, policy formulation, and control, and decentralized management of operations. An especially significant aspect of the central administration was the fact that, for performing the top executive function, it combined the capabilities, knowledge, and experience of a number of successful executives under the leadership of a man who had the capacity to lead able and aggressive men to effective cooperation. This type of administration was a far cry from the common one-man top executive of that time. Without it, so large and diversified a business could hardly have reached such a measure of success.[1]

This system was consolidated, elaborated, and greatly strengthened in the 1880's. An important step was the formation of the Standard Oil Trust. The trust agreement of 1882 established a firmer and more secure union than the alliance of the 1870's, which

[1] For a detailed description of the Standard Oil administrative organization and practices, see Ralph W. Hidy and Muriel E. Hidy, *History of Standard Oil Company (New Jersey)*, vol. I, *Pioneering in Big Business, 1882–1911* (New York, 1955).

had been held together by an interlocking system of ownership or holding of stocks and which could have been weakened at any time by the withdrawal or death of one large owner. The trust made possible the organizing of the business under separate corporations in the different states, thereby reducing the risks of crippling taxation or other handicaps under which Standard Oil of Ohio had operated outside its home state. The trust, in effect, created a type of holding organization by vesting in a self-perpetuating board of trustees the holding of the stock of corporations chartered in different states or countries and by giving the board authority and responsibility for administering the affiliated companies under rules set forth in the trust agreement.

The organization of the Standard Oil Trust was an important forward step in the development of big business. By providing a means of transcending the limitations of existing corporation law, the trust facilitated the broadening of the geographic reach of business enterprise. Other concerns followed Standard Oil's example in using the trust form of combination. Although the trust as a form of organization was weakened ten years later by a decision of the Ohio Supreme Court, New Jersey had amended its corporation statutes by that time to allow companies chartered under its laws to own the stock of other corporations. While the holding company differed in legal organization from the Trust, it provided a structure for implementing the continued use of the administrative procedures which had grown up under the Trust.

In the 1880's the trustees, who constituted the top administrative organization, were the top planners, policy makers, and coordinators for the general interest. The president was the formal head, but the executive function was shared by an executive committee of trustees. A significant administrative innovation was a system of committees of specialists (representing the principal functions and auxiliary operations) who advised and assisted the executive committee and the board of trustees.

For the particular function it represented, each committee — in close communication with both the executive committee of the Trust and executives of the operating units — had responsibility for the general planning and oversight of operations. Each committee had its own staff organization. One important staff function was to receive, collate, and analyze a constant inflow of information from all over the world about anything inside or outside Standard Oil's operations that might be of interest to the particular committee's responsibilities or to the operations it represented.

The management of operations was delegated to executives of the individual corporations; in the case of wholly-owned corporations to men chosen by the executive committee of the Trust. Each corporation was an entity in itself, but its operations were generally treated as an integral part of the whole. Exceptions were a few companies in which Standard Oil had acquired majority ownership but had not assumed control of management and with which it did not succeed in establishing close communication.

Control was exercised in various ways. Some of the trustees were members of functional committees and even presidents of important subsidiaries. Personal consultation was common — even so early, Standard Oil trustees and other executives were often traveling to consult managers of operations. Regular reporting by means of written and personal reports was extensive. An auditing organization checked financial reports of companies and worked to develop such uniformity of accounting and reporting as would make the various corporations' accounts comparable, particularly as to like functions. This was essential for the comparative studies of costs and profits that were used to determine the relative efficiency and profitability of individual corporations and of different functions. These comparisons provided essential information for guiding the executive committee in the allocation of the group's resources in "the general interest," as the men termed it.

An increasingly significant aspect of the total Standard Oil administrative process was the "consolidating, concentrating, and economizing," about which the Hidys wrote in much detail in *Pioneering in Big Business.* The trustees were interested not only in strategy and finance. While their general function was over-all planning, policy formulation, and control, they had all been operating men and several were still presidents of important operating companies. They and the functional committees set goals and standards of performance. Broad and intensive attention was given to technology, to developing new products and maintaining quality standards, to management techniques and objectives, to personnel, to a constant search for ways to decrease unit costs, and generally to establishing order and discipline in the successive operations from producing the oil to the ultimate sale of products. Everywhere emphasis was placed on realizing the economies of scale; for example, bulk methods were established in marketing, even in Europe where small-volume packaging and distribution had been the rule. The reduction of costs by more efficient methods was of course going on extensively in business in the 1880's, but, so far as we know, the comprehensiveness and scale of Standard Oil's effort was unique. Even the great British combination, Lever Brothers, was not subjected to a similar process of order and discipline until the 1920's, at the end of the long career of Lord Leverhume, its chief architect.

But with all their search for information, consultation, discussion, and careful planning, the Standard Oil executives were experimenting with a new form of business and, as we now can see, made some serious errors in policy and practices, especially in the 1870's. One error was to associate the name of Standard Oil with two marketing concerns which did not follow the combination's policies and practices. And it is at least questionable whether so aggressive a competition as theirs was necessary or wise, a matter over which there was both discussion and disagreement within Standard Oil management. Today we wonder how the Standard Oil executives could have expected to keep the ownership of "hidden companies" secret or to have escaped the prying eyes of the curious or of those with an interest in what the company did. There were no doubt good reasons for secrecy at the time, but in this matter, as, indeed, in other issues relating to competition, one is tempted to conclude that, although Standard Oil's operations had risen to a different level, its top executives were in some ways still thinking in terms of the local or regional business of their younger days.

There is evidence, however, that the executives of the combination learned from experience and criticism. They came to see certain errors, to envisage something of the broader implications of their policies, and, indeed, to recognize in a measure that a big concern could not enjoy the privacy of a small one. Yet they apparently did not come to appreciate the full extent of their break with the past, any more than their critics appreciated Standard Oil's progress beyond that past.

IV

Few would deny the efficiency and strength of Standard Oil, but many still question whether the growth of the concern was a "good" thing. Did the system in which it pioneered have broad economic value, or was it but a powerful instrument of exploitation? From an economic point of view, there can be little question but that Standard Oil made positive contributions, especially in the long run and in some respects even for the shorter term. It uniformly strove to reduce waste by increasing the scale of its operations, to increase efficiency throughout, and to bring about a closer and hence more economic coordination of successive operations. It worked to produce higher quality goods and to maintain quality in accordance with established standards, and to provide regular supplies for the market. By chemical research it made possible the manufacture of marketable products from a tremendous reserve of sulphurous Lima crude. With large storage facilities, Standard Oil also to some extent evened out the effect on the market of steep fluctuations in the volume of crude production. By reaching a larger market, it furnished an outlet for the crude production of many small producers. It provided crude oil from its pipelines for specialized refiners. And, by its aggressive marketing, it held the market for American oil against vigorous competition abroad.

But was this at too high a cost to society, even too high an economic cost, not to mention other social costs? Would consumers' prices have been even lower and other companies' profits higher if Standard Oil had been less vigorous as a competitor and if it had not attained so dominant a position? Would society have been better served if only the small specialized firms had continued to operate? In brief, would a less rapid change with a better chance of gradual adaptation to the emerging system have been better?

To answer such questions is impossible, but one can at least point to certain pertinent considerations. One might argue that Standard Oil's high profits epitomize nineteenth-century America's way of creating capital funds for the expansion of the economy. One might also observe that, in the process of economic growth and development, the destruction of submarginal firms is always taking place. The rapid rise of Standard Oil, in truth, may be looked upon as an example of what Schumpeter called creative destruction. A gradual evolution is, of course, to be desired as against a serious disruption from too rapid advance. But did not conditions in this country at the time, and indeed throughout the Western world, favor and even force rapid growth and change? In so dynamic a situation, particularly with few controls exercised on the part of government, opinion, or business itself to fit the new business institutions and operations, the race normally went to the strong.

One problem, obviously, was how to establish controls of business on this new level of enterprise. In local or even regional business systems, informal, noninstitutionalized controls, whether by public opinion or generally accepted business practice, had probably been reasonably effective. Big business rose above these, onto a kind of no-man's-land of freedom from restraint. However, big business had scarcely got under way in the oil industry before movements to curb it arose. The long and significant process of establishing government regulation is considered in Professor Johnson's paper on the development of public policy with regard to this industry.

V

Before public regulation became very effective, the oil industry generated its own counteraction to Standard Oil's strength, a development which has broad significance to the history of the evolution of business. Looked at in the long perspective of time, the dominance of the pioneer in big business in the oil industry was a transition phenomenon. Even before the combination reached its full development as an integrated concern with world-wide operations, competition arose and soon reduced Standard Oil's relative strength. It has been held commonly in the United States that the Supreme Court decision of 1911 broke the company's monopoly. This is obviously wrong, and it greatly oversimplifies and distorts what was a long-term development. Information now available shows that even in the 1880's Standard Oil began to meet strong competition in European and Oriental markets from the Nobels' Russian oil. In the 1890's Dutch East Indian oil also began to bear upon Standard's markets in the Orient; and before the end of the first decade of the twentieth century, the Royal Dutch-Shell combination had strongly challenged Standard's position in the whole Eastern Hemisphere.

In the 1890's strong competition was also taking shape at home, notably on the part of the Pure Oil group and the Mellon interests in the East. Moreover, early in the new century vigorous young companies were gathering strength based on success in oil production in California and, especially, Texas. Among the successful concerns in Texas were such companies, or their predecessors, as Gulf, Sun Oil, and Texaco. The effect of these developments at home is indicated by the fact that, whereas in 1884 Standard Oil processed about 77 per cent of the crude run by American refineries and controlled the marketing of an additional volume of products, its share of refining capacity had changed little to 1904 but by 1909 had dropped, with the advent of new fields and new refineries, to 66 per cent — this in the branch of Standard Oil's operations where it had by far the greatest comparative strength.[2]

But the rise of strong competitors did not stop the company from

[2] Hidy and Hidy, *Pioneering in Big Business*, pp. 120, 417, and 474.

expanding. Indeed, it was firm competition that made it enter the European market through wholly owned or partly owned companies, and Standard Oil's application of its techniques of aggressive bulk distribution in Europe resulted in a large increase in sales. The growth of its total operations and profits indicates a continued absolute growth, but the concern's share of the increasing oil business was falling.

There is no single explanation of the decline in Standard Oil's share of the oil industry's operations. A number of factors, obviously, had a bearing on this development.

There may have been some weakening within the company, some loss of momentum and of energy. There were, indeed, weak places in Standard's control of its widespread operations. Control seems to have been most effective in the regions and the operations in which the central administrators had the closest personal contacts. Marketing was the most difficult to handle. Salesmen have, of course, always tended to be independent, and this was just as true of companies as of individual salesmen. Standard Oil never was able to control Waters, Pierce Oil Company, a large Southwestern marketing concern which by its extreme aggressiveness and even unethical operations aroused much antagonism to the combination. That Standard Oil was attacked with special bitterness in Missouri, Texas, and Mexico was clearly more than a coincidence. In both Texas and Mexico the opposition later counted heavily against Standard Oil's developing a strong business of its own. The dissolution suit had its beginning in Missouri.

Certainly, a significant factor in the decline of Standard Oil's relative strength was the gradual reduction in the early advantages of innovation. Every one of Standard Oil's early large competitors also integrated vertically and employed mass techniques. It is significant that Russian Oil did not compete with Standard Oil in European markets until the Nobels moved into the Baku oil regions and built a large, integrated business. Royal Dutch, like the Nobels, integrated forward from production. Both these groups, it can be said, were headed by men who were superb executives and outstanding strategists. The American Pure Oil is an especially interesting case because it rose in the very region where Standard Oil was long dominant in refining and transportation. Pure Oil's base was in production; that is, it grew out of combinations of producers. But it grew beyond production by integrating as Standard Oil had done. It was able to do so in the 1890's because certain conditions were obviously more favorable to vertical integration in the Eastern part of the United States at that time than earlier; for example, railroads, although in financial distress, had ceased, because of new government regulation as well as the growth of traffic, to discriminate in rates to the extent they had earlier done. Pure Oil was also aided by a great increase in the market demand for oil, which, for example, made it economically feasible to build and operate another pipeline to seaboard. Also, Pure Oil was able to break into Standard's foreign market by joining Standard's competitors to fight the larger American company.

Standard Oil's strongest competitors, and its earliest ones, rose outside the Pennsylvania Oil Regions and had their base in producing areas which Standard Oil did not seriously try to enter at the time. The rise of those companies shows the combination's weakness in depending on a narrow base for its raw material while carrying on a world-wide marketing operation. The large production that developed in Russia and the Dutch East Indies in the 1880's and 1890's was beyond its reach. That production was not only large; it was nearer to European markets than Standard Oil's raw material source.

At home Standard's strongest competition rose in Texas, where the combination did not participate in the early development of production. For this there were several reasons. One was the strong opposition in Texas to "foreign" companies, but other out-of-state interests nevertheless early established themselves in production in what was to become the greatest oil producing state. More important, perhaps, was the local opposition to Waters, Pierce, which made any association with it suspect in the eyes of Texans. Even a more direct reason was Standard Oil's lack of the managerial resources and particularly the market outlets required for the development of additional oil production. At the time when Texas was in its first surge of oil development Standard was nearly swamped with the problems it met in taking care of its own production and the oil of its pipeline connections in the Mid-Continent and in California.

Another factor favoring the rise of competitors was the appearance of new products in the manufacture and sale of which Standard Oil was handicapped by its earlier commitment to kerosene. Kerosene was the first product for which there had been a sufficient demand to make possible Standard Oil's mass operations, and it continued to be the combination's most important product. The combination had also acquired a considerable market for lubricants and industrial fuels. But as a matter of policy, it had from the first left products with a limited, or local, demand to other companies. The Texas producers succeeded in developing a new demand, one that had not appeared in the industry in any significant way outside California. Texas crudes proved especially suitable for manufacturing heavy fuel oils. The Texas refiners looked for a new market and found it near at hand in the fueling of locomotives and ships.

Similarly, the increasing demand for gasoline, with the rapid rise in the number of automobiles in Europe and the United States, gave Standard's competitors a striking new market opportunity. Not only was this a market in which Standard Oil had not acquired a strong position; it was also one in which the company for some time was handicapped by not having sufficient light crudes for the manufacture of a larger per cent of its output in gasoline, instead of kerosene, to be economically advantageous. The Royal Dutch was especially fortunate in its large supply of light Sumatran crudes, which enabled it to obtain a strong position in the European market — and even to enter the United States market in 1912. Within our country, The Texas Company, which was not handicapped by heavy capital investments in the manufacture and sale of kerosene, moved fast to pre-empt the gasoline market by entering into retailing in a strong way. By integrating forward into the consumers' market, it beat Standard in gaining a strong position in the great market of the future.

A factor of considerable importance in the rise of Standard Oil's competitors, particularly at home, was the failure of the combination not only to expand into new areas but also to seize developing market opportunities. Even Standard's financial resources, strong as they were, were probably not strong enough to finance expansion commensurate with the growth of the industry, but the rapid expansion that the company was undergoing strained its administrative resources and its operating management. As for entering upon the manufacture and sale of new products, its whole system was occupied with its traditional product lines. Standard was suffering from the fate that has normally overtaken pioneers in industrial development, that of being tied by earlier investments and operations.

Although economic factors were the governing ones in the rise of competition, even within the domestic industry public opinion and government regulation were not without their effect before 1911. Standard Oil's executives were sensitive to criticism; as one wrote, they craved the confidence and respect of honorable men. In the 1880's, after their first strong thrust to expand and after their struggle with other strong groups had been won, they began to heed criticism and to weigh their own practices and policies more critically. How far this affected their operations is not clear. More obvious is the result of attacks in courts and the threat of such attacks. Antitrust and price regulation by states was effective before the impact of the decision of 1911. Standard's legal counsel who joined the combination in 1881 — S. C. T. Dodd — urged conformity not only with the letter but also with the spirit of the law. There is some reason to believe that, because of the mounting attacks on Standard Oil, its executives felt the effects of both the letter and the spirit more strongly at that time than did its competitors.

Before the Supreme Court decree of 1911 dissolved the Standard Oil combination, competition in the oil industry had established itself on the level of large-scale, integrated operations. No company had come to equal the strength of Standard Oil but several were highly dynamic and were aggressively challenging it in many markets. This does not mean that the whole industry was occupied by these large concerns or that they dominated all parts of it. The small operators and the larger specialists were still of importance in most operations. However, the over-all planners and coordinators, the big risk-takers were the larger integrated companies. Big business had changed the early oil industry of regionally oriented specialists to one better structured to supply the tremendous world-wide market for oil products that had developed in the life span of one generation of executives.

Public Policy and Concentration in the Petroleum Industry 1870-1911

by Arthur M. Johnson

HARVARD BUSINESS SCHOOL

INTRODUCTION

The petroleum industry has the dubious distinction of being intimately involved in the development of national public policy with respect to big business. One need only mention the Interstate Commerce Act, the Sherman Act, the Elkins Act, the Bureau of Corporations, and the "Rule of Reason" to recall that the oil industry was connected with these various efforts to deal with concentrated economic power by: regulation, prohibition, publicity, and administrative and judicial discretion. Behind these efforts at the national level was a long series of comparable efforts at the state level. I would like to discuss early problems of concentration in the industry from this standpoint.

When the historian turns to questions of public policy, there is a basic difference between his approach and that of the economist. The historian is interested in *how* and *why* a policy came to be what it was at any given time *in the past*. He is therefore interested in the past interaction between business decisions and the formulation and administration of public policy. He is interested in continuums. He recognizes that the cumulative impact of decisions — large and small — made by businessmen and government officials creates a framework for the solution of future problems from which it is extremely difficult to escape. In short, he recognizes — and, if you will, accepts — the lag that develops between changing economic conditions, especially with reference to business structure and behavior, and the adoption of public policies intended to deal with them. In attempting to understand such developments he may not be able to avoid rendering judgments, but he can strive for balance; he is not concerned with forgiving or condemning but with *understanding* why men acted as they did in the past.

The economist, I would suggest, has other and equally legitimate interests. He tends to be more interested in *current* public policy. He is not so interested in why and how a policy got to be what it is, but in what is "wrong" with it from society's standpoint. As a result, he is frequently more sanguine about the possibilities of changing it than is the historian. Because the human element is not a central concern of economic theory or quantitative studies, the economist may also misjudge the possibilities of institutional change, and be less cautious than the historian in condemning men's motives and behavior. The assumption, or theoretical proof, that there can be an optimum allocation of resources in a society may make it difficult for him to refrain from such judgments.

The assertion is sometimes made that for business historians "to understand is to forgive." [1] Actually neither condemnation nor forgiveness is the proper concern of the business historian. Therefore, if in analyzing the early history of the petroleum industry I mistake the "was" for the "ought," it is not the product of a conscious design but of my own inability to achieve the objectivity that I advocate.

THE ORIGIN AND NATURE OF CONCENTRATION

Before examining the consequences of concentration, it is first necessary to say a little about the process of concentration. The petroleum industry of 1870 came close to exemplifying the econ-

---

[1] See Gabriel Kolko, "The Premises of Business Revisionism," *Business History Review*, vol. XXXIII (Autumn, 1959), pp. 330–344.

omist's model of pure competition: many buyers and sellers dealing in a homogeneous product, where price could not be appreciably affected by any one of them, and with free entry and exit in response to economic forces. Production of crude oil was localized in western Pennsylvania and in the hands of numerous producers, none of whom could individually affect its price by varying his output. Conditions in refining were comparable. In 1870 there were 155 refineries, 94 of them located in Pennsylvania.[2] The major product, kerosene, was essentially undifferentiated and involved a widely available and relatively unsophisticated technology. Although the number of refineries had declined from 300 in 1863 as the scale of refining operations increased, one could still enter the field on a competitive basis for an investment of $60,000 to $80,000.[3] As for transportation, there were numerous pipelines to haul or store oil between the well and the railhead or refinery. Railroad competition for oil freights to refineries outside the Oil Region was fierce. In distribution, there were numerous jobbers and wholesalers available. There were no artificial barriers to entry at any level of the industry and no affirmative public policies which restrained the tactics or nature of competition.

Given this situation, instability — not equilibrium as we should have expected from the economist's model — resulted. Specialization by function and a lack of balance between functions resulted in a competitive scramble that at times verged on chaos. In the early 1870's market forces were determining prices and output of the petroleum industry, but at the cost of wastefulness in production, duplication in pipeline gathering systems, discriminations in freight rates, and substantial excess refining capacity. Theory might lead one to believe that these were short-run costs which the free play of market forces would eliminate, but theory necessarily ignores the resourcefulness of businessmen in extricating themselves from the grip of the "invisible hand." Given the structure of the petroleum industry with production, transportation, and refining in different hands, the effort to eliminate the uncertain and uneven impact of market forces could begin at any level and proceed by voluntary agreement, horizontal combination, or vertical integration.

Voluntary associational activity flourished at all levels of the industry. On the producers' level it ranged from partnership and corporation alliances in drilling to a general Petroleum Producers' Association. In pipelining four major groups emerged, three of them

[2] Harold F. Williamson and Arnold R. Daum, *The American Petroleum Industry: The Age of Illumination, 1859–1899* (Evanston, Ill., 1959), p. 471.
[3] *Ibid.*, p. 282.

allied with either the Erie or the Pennsylvania Railroad. Refiners in Philadelphia and Pittsburgh pooled their resources and turned to commission houses to help them achieve economies in purchasing crude oil and in selling finished products. Other oilmen attempted independently to extend their markets by cutting price and to reduce unit costs by combining functions.[4] Still, as the Pittsburgh *Commercial* observed, during 1871 the petroleum industry in all its branches had found the business a "losing one."[5]

In Cleveland, John D. Rockefeller and his associates in the newly formed Standard Oil Company of Ohio approached the problem of instability via the route of horizontal combination. A tightly knit group of refiners could not only achieve economies in that end of the business but could bring pressure to bear to reduce transportation costs which represented as much as 20 per cent of the final product cost. There is no need here to recount the success of their efforts in terms of the development of the Standard Oil combination, integrating backward to pipelines, forward to marketing, and culminating in the trust agreement of 1882 and near-monopoly in pipeline transportation and refining. This success reflected first-rate managerial ability, the reduction of unit costs, the improvement and diversification of products, and innovations in corporate structure and physical facilities.[6]

It is no derogation of these positive achievements, however, to maintain that Standard Oil's predominance also rested on its power to block entry to refining and marketing by the exercise of its power over transportation between the center of crude production and major consuming areas. It did so first by exploiting the rivalries of trunk-line railroads engaged in a larger struggle for East-West traffic, by pitting water transportation against rail, and later by control of trunk pipelines, augmented by agreements to maintain pipeline rates at railroad levels. By the mid-1880's, the existence of competition at the refining and marketing levels was more a matter of tolerance than necessity.

As I see it, after 1877, when Standard Oil overcame the challenge to its position in refining by the Pennsylvania Railroad-Empire pipeline alliance, the problems of concentration in the refining and marketing end of the petroleum industry in the last analysis hinged on

[4] See Ralph W. Hidy and Muriel E. Hidy, *Pioneering in Big Business, 1882–1911* (New York, 1955), pp. 9–13.
[5] Quoted in Arthur M. Johnson, *The Development of American Petroleum Pipelines* (Ithaca, 1956), pp. 17–18.
[6] See Hidy and Hidy, *Pioneering in Big Business*, pp. 14–121; Williamson and Daum, *American Petroleum Industry*, pp. 343–551 *passim*.

the combination's power over transportation.[7] Lewis Emery, Jr., inveterate foe of Standard Oil and himself a successful oilman, told the Industrial Commission in 1899 that "They [S. O.] have got nothing better in any of their works than I have got in mine, except it be, perhaps, in their fine laboratories, in the manufacture of residuums or the by-products." In his view, "The whole question is the question of transportation."[8] While the latter statement is subject to such important qualifications as those already mentioned, the most recent analysts of the industry during this period reach a conclusion that is not inconsistent with Emery's. Williamson and Daum conclude that "had railroads been able or willing to treat all shippers alike and, had trunk pipelines been able to develop as common carriers under effective governmental supervision, it is at least questionable whether Standard could ever have controlled such a large share of the oil business. It is further reasonable to suppose that with greater freedom of entry, other entrepreneurs would have built up organizations sufficiently large at the refining and possibly the marketing level to achieve economies of scale."[9]

A corollary to this analysis seems to be that if — and it is a big IF — public policy had been different, the structure of the industry might well have been different. Concentration of control over oil transportation developed under a public policy of *laissez faire*, and I would now like to examine why positive public policies failed to provide an answer to this key problem of concentration in the oil industry.

Public Policy as a Tactical, Competitive Weapon

In speaking of public policy, I mean an exercise of governmental power — state or national — which explicitly or implicitly, positively or negatively, seeks to promote goals deemed to be in the "public interest." In practice, of course, public policy is not framed in a vacuum, conceptions of the public interest vary, and in application — or lack thereof — a statutory expression of the public interest may represent a public policy quite different from the one envisaged at the time of its enactment into law.

I have already suggested that there are different ways of looking at public policy affecting business. One way is to measure it against a yardstick representing certain objective and presumably desirable

[7] For an analysis of this contest, see Johnson, *American Pipelines*, pp. 49–69.
[8] United States Industrial Commission, *Reports of the Industrial Commission*, 19 vols. (Washington, 1901–1903), vol. I, p. 633.
[9] Williamson and Daum, *American Petroleum Industry*, p. 729.

criteria (from society's standpoint) of economic structure and performance. Another way is to examine the pragmatic process by which public policy is made and applied to business. I am concerned only with the latter area in this paper.

Pragmatically, public policy offers an outdistanced competitor a competitive weapon if he can succeed in having it applied only to a rival. But used in this way it is primarily a tactical weapon. The strategic weapons consist of productive facilities, managerial know-how, and the other elements of enterprise with which a businessman can battle his rival for the customer's dollar. Public policy used as a tactical weapon can prepare the scene and affect the employment of strategic weapons, but it cannot win a war by itself. Oilmen sometimes lost sight of the difference in attacking Standard Oil.

The first conscious efforts to formulate public policy with respect to oil transportation came as a competitive tactic from within the oil industry. From the very first major episode in Standard Oil's rise to power — the South Improvement Company — its opponents turned to the state for aid.[10] In seeking to shape the formulation and application of public policy with respect to oil transportation over the next twenty years, it seems to me that they had two main tactical goals: one was to improve the opportunities for competition at the refining and marketing levels by both positive and negative means; the other was simply to punish the oil combination for its success. The line between the two was elastic and frequently quite confused. Given the general public's indifference toward the internal structure of a new industry, formulation of specific public policies affecting it was necessarily the work of interested parties. How did they discharge this responsibility?

PUBLIC POLICY AND ECONOMIC SELF-INTEREST

In seeking to use public policy in the attack on concentration, there were two focal points of effort by the independents: railroads and pipelines. With respect to railroads their primary effort was to prevent rate discriminations. With respect to pipelines their primary effort was to obtain the right of eminent domain so they could lay the pipes and get the economic advantages of the new medium.

In the Pennsylvania legislature, oil producers fought a losing battle against the Pennsylvania Railroad during the 1870's. By turning to pipelines the oilmen sought to escape the railroad's grip,

[10] See Johnson, *American Pipelines*, pp. 17–25.

but in constructing the lines they found themselves continually blocked by the railroad's opposition. They made continuing demands for the right of eminent domain for pipelines, but they obtained only a limited law in 1872 and had to wait until 1883 for a general one. As far as I know, in the 1870's they sponsored only one bill to regulate pipelines as common carriers, and it was defeated in the 1875 legislative session.[11] From at least 1876 on, however, they actively sought federal regulation of railroads to put an end to rate discriminations.[12] In this drive there was no attempt to include pipelines.

In moving onto the national stage, independent oilmen could tap a source of strength that had far wider roots than the Oil Region by fitting their case against railroads into the growing stream of public criticism of the railroads' discriminatory practices. Even more important from their point of view was the fact that governmental regulation of railroads did not threaten any interests in the oil industry other than Standard Oil's preferential position. Some independents went so far as to advocate government ownership of railroads, while the idea of federal regulation of pipelines apparently never even occurred to them.[13]

By following the most obvious path of short-run economic self-interest, however, the independents made a major mistake if, as I suggest, the key to the concentration problem lay in transportation. Because independents regarded public policy as a tactical rather than strategic weapon, they failed to press unitedly for a state or federal common carrier pipeline law when it might have placed a major restraint on Standard Oil at little cost to themselves. Both the free pipeline law in Pennsylvania and the federal Interstate Commerce Act for which they worked, came too late to change the picture of concentration. Standard Oil had already the major trunk pipeline system. The prohibition of railroad rate discriminations under these circumstances offered little relief since bulk crude oil shipments were largely going by pipe.[14] The right to

---

[11] See Johnson, *American Pipelines*, pp. 41–48. Free pipeline bills carried the implication of common carrier status for pipelines obtaining a route by exercising the right of eminent domain, but this aspect of the proposed legislation generally received little attention.

[12] The 1876 effort originated with Pittsburgh refining interests adversely affected by railroad agreements that favored Cleveland. In 1878 the Petroleum Producers' Union took up the fight.

[13] Among oilmen, Lewis Emery, Jr., became a leading advocate of government ownership of railroads as an answer to the carriers' discriminatory practices. David Kirk of the Producers' Protective Association suggested state ownership of pipelines in 1888. Again, however, such suggestions — and they were little more — were primarily tactical approaches to the transportation problem.

[14] In 1888 railroads carried only 28 per cent of the crude shipped to points also served by pipeline. Williamson and Daum, *American Petroleum Industry*, p. 457.

condemn land for pipeline construction was not in itself — and never had been — an answer to the formidable concentration of refining, marketing, financial and transportation power. However, had common carrier status been forced on pipelines by federal action in 1887 or earlier, Standard Oil might have had one of its major strategic weapons neutralized: both as a barrier to entry and as a major source of revenue.

Public Policy as a Punitive Weapon

Frustrated at almost every turn, the independents turned to another tactical approach: using the power of government to punish Standard Oil. Under the pressure of declining prices resulting from overproduction, the producers in 1878 applied to the executive branch of the Pennsylvania government for legal action against Standard's United Pipe Lines and the oil-carrying railroads. While these cases moved slowly, the producers added to them in 1879 by instigating a conspiracy suit against Rockefeller and leading members of the combination, charging conspiracy to monopolize the buying and selling of crude oil, extorting unreasonable rebates and commissions, and similar offenses. In 1880 Standard Oil offered to settle out of court by discontinuing the objectionable practices, though not binding itself rigidly. The producers, split as usual, decided to accept the offer. Thus ended one phase of their effort to punish Standard Oil.

Meanwhile, an effort to compete with the combination through construction of a trunk pipeline to the seaboard proved the feasibility of such lines, but the backers lacked the resources and the determination to keep the refineries on which they depended out of Standard Oil's hands. The Tide Water Pipe Line, however, showed that innovation could breach Standard Oil's power over transportation — a lesson that the combination quickly turned to its own use. The Tide Water threat was neutralized and Standard trunk pipelines were pushed to the seaboard.

In 1887 the producers were again suffering the consequences of overproduction. The free pipeline law of 1883 had not produced the anticipated results; railroad discriminations continued. Therefore, they once again supported punitive action against the combination. This time it took the form of a bill that vowed in its title that it was intended to "punish" corporations which did not conform to its provisions. Among the original provisions were requirements for pipelines to connect with any well upon application, accept all oil offered, store it for at least a year, and submit to regulation of charges.[15] Although the most unreasonable parts of the bill were stricken by the time it passed the Pennsylvania House, there remained a sufficient diversity of interests involved to bring about its defeat in the Senate. Again Standard Oil made some limited concessions to satisfy the producers. Faced with a flood of oil, both groups found common ground. Bilateral monopoly temporarily replaced monopoly.

The independents' last effort in Pennsylvania to use the power of the state to punish Standard Oil came in 1891 with the Burdick bill, which bore a strong resemblance to the 1887 proposal. However, the same lack of unity which had helped to defeat the earlier bill was operative in the case of the new one. As a result, it failed even to win a place on the legislative calendar. The *Parker Phoenix* summed it up when it commented: [16]

> It seems to a fellow up a tree, that the producers are not united on any particular measure, and as yet are still blinded by the immense success attained by the transportation company; namely, the Standard. Whenever the producers shall become blind to outside interests and will pursue unitedly their own business, then, and then only, will the desired end be attained.

Even had the producers been united, only federal — not state — action could have provided the relief they sought.

By this time, the producers who had been most active in using public policy as a tactical weapon against Standard Oil were turning more determinedly to pipelines, pipeline innovation, and integrated operations as strategic weapons. Combining with independent Oil Region refiners, they built up the Pure Oil combination which, with the aid of the first products trunk line, successfully resisted the efforts of the railroads and Standard Oil to repel its challenge.[17] Meanwhile the center of crude oil production had been moving out of Pennsylvania, and one of the prime conditions of Standard Oil's early control of transportation was disappearing. With the opening of the Texas fields, a flock of new integrated companies patterned after Standard Oil soon changed the monopoly picture into one of oligopoly.[18] However, the new companies could not

[15] For an analysis of the measure, see Johnson, *American Pipelines*, pp. 130–137; Williamson and Daum, *American Petroleum Industry*, pp. 558–562.
[16] Quoted in *Oil City Derrick*, Feb. 28, 1891.
[17] Why Pure Oil succeeded where Tide Water had failed is a fascinating problem, susceptible to economic, motivational, and organizational explanations.
[18] It is interesting to speculate how the structure of the early industry would have differed had oil been discovered in Texas in 1859 rather than in Pennsylvania. While this is not an historical question, it does suggest the significance of the geographical factor in making transportation a key to the concentration problem as the industry actually developed.

escape the inheritance that earlier industry efforts to use public policy as a tactical weapon had bequeathed to them.

Public Policy and the "Public Interest"

In turning to public policy, oilmen had been grasping a double-edged sword. While their intention was for it to cut only one way — at Standard Oil — it could just as well be used against them. By attempting to identify the public interest with their self-interest, the industry opponents of Standard Oil had helped to put in motion forces which they could not control. By focusing on railroad discriminations, for example, they aided passage of the Interstate Commerce Act. While it came too late to affect the picture of concentration in the oil industry, it established a precedent for future government regulation of all business. Popular hostility to Standard Oil, fanned by writers like Henry Demarest Lloyd who was all too willing to accept the producers' charges against the oil combination, likewise aided passage of the Sherman Antitrust Act.[19] However, with the industry relying more on strategic weapons of enterprise than on tactical weapons of public policy, no oilman sought to invoke the federal act against Standard Oil. Lewis Emery, Jr., the most ardent advocate of public policy as a tactical weapon, called the Sherman Act "one of the best laws ever written," [20] but he preferred to make his challenge to Standard Oil by enterprise.

It is important to keep in mind that the industry's complaints against Standard Oil preceded and accompanied the beginnings of a major merger movement in American industry which caused mounting concern to the American people. This concern reflected the glaring inequalities of wealth that accompanied the rise of big business, the obvious threat to democratic control of economic life, the apparent barriers to new enterprise, and the exercise of economic power governed primarily by self-interest. Journalists and politicians, drawing on evidence and allegations against Standard Oil provided by the rest of the industry over a score of years, made the trust the symbol of all that was bad in the new combination movement.

Economists, on the other hand, were less ready to condemn combinations or even Standard Oil. With a certain amount of exaggeration, George Stigler has observed, "Economists as wise as

---

[19] While Congress was considering the Sherman Act, Rockefeller felt it necessary to defend publicly the Standard Oil Trust. Williamson and Daum, *American Petroleum Industry*, pp. 706–707.
[20] *Reports of the Industrial Commission*, vol. I, p. 671.

Taussig, as incisive as Fisher, as fond of competition as Clark and Fetter, insisted upon discussing the [merger] movement largely or exclusively in terms of industrial evolution and the economies of scale . . . . One must regretfully record that in this period Ida Tarbell and Henry Demarest Lloyd did more than the American Economic Association to foster the policy of competition." [21] This view finds support in a contemporary review of literature on the trust problem. Charles J. Bullock in 1901 found that no less than five books and a "decided majority" of the articles published at the turn of the century accepted the trust movement as inevitable, arising out of destructive competition and realizing economies through the combination of capital and skilled management. He cited Lloyd's *Wealth against Commonwealth* as typical of another class of writer who attributed the growth of trusts to special favors and other abuses, such as the "smokeless rebate." [22] It was this school, by emphasizing morality rather than economics, that finally succeeded in arousing public opinion against concentrated economic power to the point where public policy became a political rather than an industry weapon.

Public interest in federal action with respect to the oil industry was rooted in questions of ethics more than structure, and legislative proposals were framed with reference to a structure that was already undergoing a transformation. The pipeline amendment to the Hepburn Act in 1906 is a case in point. It was designed to make pipelines common carriers subject to federal regulation, but the proposal came from Senator Lodge of Massachusetts rather than from any representative of the oil country. While the pipeline amendment was a minor part of a larger administration strategy to strengthen the Interstate Commerce Act, the Lodge proposal reflected primarily a consumer rather than industry interest. Accompanying this proposal was another one that would have incidentally — rather than as a primary purpose — divorced pipelines from other parts of the industry. The mood of Congress is shown by Senator Cullom's recollection of the first conference on this measure. He reported that "It was not discussed except to agree generally that whatever would curb Standard Oil we ought to be for." [23] The confusion and conflicting goals of the legislators were reflected in Senator Elkins' declaration that "What we wish to do

---

[21] George Stigler, "Monopoly and Oligopoly by Merger," *American Economic Review,* vol. XL, No. 2 (May, 1950), pp. 30–31.

[22] Charles J. Bullock, "Trust Literature: a Survey and a Criticism," *The Quarterly Journal of Economics,* vol. XV (Feb., 1901), pp. 167–217.

[23] *Congressional Record,* 59th Cong., 1st Sess. (June 25, 1906), pp. 9108–9109.

is to improve conditions, stop abuses, prevent monopolies, but not to injure any interest doing business in the country." [24] In the face of protests from the industry, therefore, pipeline divorcement was dropped but common carrier status was imposed. If the *Congressional Record* is any guide, it seems that the senators were not clear on what they were doing about the oil industry but they felt that they must do something. It is equally clear that conditions in the industry itself had changed to the point where the weapons of enterprise were making headway against concentration and in this struggle the industry felt that it now had more to fear than to hope from public policy.

The subsequent record of enforcement of the pipeline amendment showed that new integrated concerns were as reluctant as Standard Oil to accept the legal imposition of common carrier status, which they felt to be at odds with the actual economic function of their pipelines.[25]

Speaking at the National Civic Federation Conference on Trusts in 1907, F. W. Taussig of Harvard gave an economist's support to this view by stating his thesis that combinations reflected economies of scale and that legislation challenging economic reality would be futile. Said Taussig: [26]

> Whatever may have been the artificial causes of the origin and early development of the oil monopoly, through the manipulation of railway rates and the helplessness of railways in competition with each other, the tendency toward single management and ownership seems to me to have become inevitable with the pipe line. Legislation may provide that pipe lines shall be common carriers, and rival pipe lines may be encouraged. Yet this stage in the mechanical development of the industry seems to me to make combination inevitable. Sooner or later rival pipe lines will combine, the industry necessarily will come under the control of those owning the unique transportation facilities, the common carrier provision will prove illusory.

Obviously by this time the industry had already proved that there was room for more than one pipeline system and the fact that combination accompanied the initial development of trunk pipelines does not necessarily prove a casual connection. In the absence of common carrier legislation, however, effective competition with Standard Oil demanded integration and once this was accomplished, the new concerns had reason to present a united front with Standard

[24] *Ibid.* (June 26, 1906), pp. 9250–9252.
[25] See *The Pipe Line Cases*, 234 U. S. 548 (1914).
[26] *Proceedings of the National Conference on Trusts and Combinations Under the Auspices of the National Civic Federation, Chicago, October 25–27, 1907* (New York, 1908), p. 377.

Oil against pipeline regulation and/or divorcement. In any event, partially as a result of the industry's own earlier efforts, the government in 1906 claimed jurisdiction over interstate oil pipelines and divorcement by federal action has remained a potential threat to the industry ever since.

During this period there was a noticeable ambivalence of public and governmental attitudes toward big business. In theory and in practice, economists, legislators, judges, and consumers could see benefits in combination; yet they were equally aware of abuses and disadvantages of the type already mentioned.

As a superb politician and forceful chief executive, Theodore Roosevelt embodied perfectly the ambivalence of popular attitudes toward big business. He never ceased to stress the importance of big business to the economy, but he distinguished between "good" and "bad" combinations on a subjective basis. He found in Standard Oil an ideal whipping boy to achieve his legislative and political ends. Thus, he exploited Standard Oil's opposition to a Bureau of Corporations in order to obtain congressional approval of this executive organ of publicity about business. Subsequently, in attempting to strengthen the Interstate Commerce Act, he found good use for a Bureau report that castigated Standard's relations with the railroads. Finally, he found in the Bureau's investigation of the oil industry sufficient grounds to justify an antitrust suit against the oil combination. His primary emphasis was on Standard's behavior, which he compared with a system of morality that would justify everything from ballot-box stuffing to murder. At the same time, he condemned the literal language of the Sherman Act as running counter to the economic forces of the age and asked for executive and administrative discretion in dealing with big business.[27]

The ambivalence of popular attitudes toward big business was also reflected in a transition by the Supreme Court from an inconsistent insistence that atomistic competition was the goal of national policy to acceptance of "reasonable" combinations as being in the public interest. Roosevelt's bid to institutionalize executive distinctions between "good" and "bad" combinations was rejected. The Court made itself the arbiter of such questions in the Standard Oil case, where the company was found guilty but the rule of reason was introduced as a yardstick for future interpretation of the antitrust law.

Significantly, Chief Justice White for the majority in this case

[27] See Arthur M. Johnson, "Theodore Roosevelt and the Bureau of Corporations," *Mississippi Valley Historical Review*, vol. XLV (March, 1959), pp. 571–590.

emphasized that the purpose and intent of Standard Oil to maintain dominance in the industry was revealed by its method of organization "in the absence of countervailing circumstances." Corroboration was found in "the slow but resistless methods . . . by which means of transportation were absorbed and brought under control [and] the system of marketing which was adopted . . . ." Control over the refined product, the Court held, gave the combination, of necessity, "substantial power over the crude product." [28]

CONCLUSION

It seems quite clear that positive public policy lagged behind the problems of concentration in the oil industry with which it was intended to deal. The electorate and its representatives were slow to perceive the significance of these problems — partly because they were complex, partly because they were new, and partly because members of the industry suffered under these same handicaps and in turning to public policy defined the problems of concentration in terms of their own short-run self-interest. As a result, positive public policy adapted to rather than shaped the early development of the oil industry. I think the same thing may be said with respect to the rise of other industries which wrought a major transformation in the structure of American industry in the period between the Civil War and World War I. It was not accidental, however, that the oil industry was in the forefront at each major step of this process of adjusting the relationship between the public interest and private economic interests. The oil industry had led the way toward industrial combination, and intra-industry conflict influenced the course of public policy in dealing with the new phenomenon.

In the oil industry the immediate answer to the problems of concentration came in the first decade of this century through changing conditions and through enterprise. The statutory expression of public policy emerging from this early period remains. The process of adjustment between private and public interests continues, challenging the historian's efforts to understand the present in the light of the past and the economist's efforts to analyze and evaluate the present with a view to the future.

[28] *Standard Oil Company of New Jersey et al.* v. *The United States,* 221 U. S. 1 (1911), pp. 75–77.

The
Value of Business History
in the Search for Oil

by Wallace E. Pratt

STANDARD OIL COMPANY (NEW JERSEY),
RETIRED

It is for me an extraordinary privilege to participate in this Seminar on the History of the Petroleum Industry in its centennial year. But along with this sense of privilege I am aware also of a certain uneasiness, because here I venture to speak on a subject — business history — with which I am by no means familiar. My experience in business is limited to a single industry — petroleum. Within the petroleum industry my activities have always been confined to one function — exploration. And, although my professional career has extended over a period of 50 years, my whole contact with business history consists of a single brief encounter. Clearly, I cannot presume to pass judgment on the value of business history to businessmen generally.

My first awareness of business history came to me during the years immediately preceding the last world war. As a member of the executive committee of Jersey Standard Oil at that time, I shared in the deliberations which eventually resulted in a decision to compile a comprehensive business history of that corporation. Practically from its inception Jersey Standard Oil had been heavily engaged in foreign trade. Yet the decision of our committee really grew out of the virtual failure of our efforts to defend commercial arrangements into which we had entered many years earlier with a chemical firm in Germany.

These arrangements involved an exchange of patents and information covering the preparation of liquid hydrocarbons from coal and heavy oil by a process of hydrogenation. In the early 1920's when this joint research with the Germans first began, leaders in the American Petroleum Industry were alarmed at the steadily dwindling domestic reserves of crude oil, and it had seemed important to us to be able to make liquid fuels by adding hydrogen to coal or to heavy oil. Between 1928 and 1939 we worked diligently with our German associates, and out of this work we developed many products which were to be of vast importance later in our own conduct of the war. Among these products were hundred octane aviation gasoline, synthetic rubber, and toluene for the manufacture of TNT.

After Pearl Harbor, however, in an atmosphere of war hysteria, well-meaning but misguided patriots interpreted the fact that we had these commercial arrangements with a German organization as evidence that we were pro-German. And, to our dismay, we found ourselves utterly unable to convince these critics of the facts. Our frustration reached its climax when, at the close of a long hearing in Washington at which we attempted to place our record before a congressional committee, the chairman of that committee, reporting to the Press, exclaimed: "This is treason!"

We finally realized that we simply did not possess complete and unimpeachable records of all our relationships with the Germans. Gradually it dawned on us that it would have been extremely helpful if we had been in position to show our critics a comprehensive history of our long business career — in Germany and elsewhere — prepared by a competent, completely detached independent agency given free access to all records and authorized in advance to make and publish its own findings. Such a record, we concluded, would surely have strengthened our defense.

The early debates of our committee on the wisdom of preserving a complete record of company operations in the form of a business history revealed a considerable reluctance among our members to make public all our past actions and decisions. Would not such a record facilitate hostile court action against us? We hesitated, but we soon crossed this bridge. We recalled the deeply critical climate of opinion against the Standard Oil group which prevailed in this country at the time the dissolution decree was entered in 1911. Beyond question, we felt, this attitude was intensified by the sensational charges of Ida M. Tarbell and others which were then widely current and familiar to the public.

If this same public, we asked ourselves, had had access to an objective, unimpeachable record of the facts, such as an independently compiled business history of our company might have afforded, would not that record have tempered the prevailing unfriendly sentiment toward the old Standard Oil Trust and the successor Standard Oil group? Our own knowledge of our record made us confident that the interests of the Standard Oil of those days would have been greatly served if there had been available to everyone a completely candid and comprehensive business history of the company, extending back to the very date of its charter.

The dearth of accurate factual data on the true character of American business enterprise over the last half century and the one-sided nature of the published comment with which business was confronted during that period have been emphasized recently by two different writers, Harold F. Williamson and Stanley Pargellis.[1] Pargellis has listed the titles of what have been described as "The Fundamental Sources of American History." For the period during which Standard Oil was under most violent attack this list included the following significant titles: Resolutions of the National Grange; The Preamble of the Constitution of the Knights of Labor; The Platform of the Populist Party; and William Jennings Bryan's Cross of Gold speech. Nowhere in this whole collection of "Fundamental Sources of American History," Pargellis observes, is there a single document which presents "the attitudes, the arguments, the economic and political philosophy of businessmen."

---

[1] Harold F. Williamson, *The Professors Discover American Business* (Evanston, Ill.). Stanley Pargellis, "The Judgment of History on American Business," a Newcomen Address (Chicago, 1943), p. 10. Quoted by Williamson, *American Business*.

From these comments the climate of opinion against which the old Standard Oil group attempted to defend itself may be clearly discerned. It was the contemplation of this record, coupled with the hostility of a similarly uninformed and prejudiced (as we judged it to be) public opinion at the beginning of the Second World War, which finally convinced Jersey Standard Oil of its dire need for an accurate, impartial, and comprehensive company history.

So it has come about that my experience, meager as it may be as a basis for broad judgment, has convinced me that for the executive in the oil business and for the corporation he serves, an adequate business history is an asset of great potential value. I have come, in short, to rate as indispensable to the successful oilman a thorough knowledge of the history of the corporation he directs. I would even apply to business history especially the terse summary with which a contemporary historian, who recommended the study of general history to a group of businessmen, concluded his argument. "History," he said, "cannot make a businessman clever in his business decisions; but in providing him perspective — in providing him with an imaginative understanding of the social origins and consequences of what he is doing — it offers the businessman wisdom." [2]

At this point it may be pertinent to recall that, of the four members of Jersey Standard Oil's executive committee which first proposed the compilation of a history of that company, only one is alive today — 20 years after the event. So rapidly does business become history, whether or not that history be preserved. Some such reflection as this may have moved Montaigne when he declared: "The only good histories are written by those who had command in the events they describe."

But I wish to look in particular at my own sector of the petroleum industry — oilfinding. Does a study of business history offer the oilfinder a perspective which may bring him wisdom?

It has been my good fortune to witness an almost incredible achievement over the last 50 years of the art of prospecting based on the science of geology. Despite a constantly mounting demand for liquid fuels, a demand which has multiplied some tenfold, both in our own country and in the rest of the free world, discovery has more than kept pace with consumption. Geologists and oilfinders generally are justly proud of this accomplishment. It is the more re-

[2] W. Woodruff, "History and the Businessman," *The Business History Review* (Sept., 1956), p. 259.

markable in that throughout this period our best-informed authorities have repeatedly expressed alarm at the paucity of our worldwide petroleum resources, and have predicted their imminent exhaustion.

Nevertheless, when the record of oilfinding is analyzed, disturbing anomalies appear. Currently we celebrate the centennial of the founding of the American Petroleum Industry. Our search for new oilfields in this country began almost as soon as our first discovery attained its full development. Promptly this search became effective. Within a few years new oilfields had rewarded the efforts of one prospector after another. The basic principle involved in the art of prospecting for oil — the anticlinal theory — was conceived and announced to the geological fraternity very soon after the problem first presented itself. Through all the ensuing years this same principle has guided our search, as it does today. It is still entirely adequate for our purposes. We have sharpened our prospecting tools and devised marvelously effective new tools and techniques but the guiding principle remains unchanged. Yet, more than 70 years were to pass before we discovered the greatest of all our oilfields in the United States — East Texas. And a still longer period elapsed before we found the greatest oilfield we know on earth — Kuwait in the Middle East.

Neither East Texas nor Kuwait is deeply buried or obscurely hidden, as oilfields go. The art of oilfinding has long been adequate to guide us unerringly to either of them. Why, then, in the frantic search for oil all over the earth — a search which has been perhaps the principal concern of the petroleum industry throughout its history — have these rather conspicuous, giant oilfields escaped detection for so long? Why, if, as we think, we have known all along how to find oilfields, have our most significant discoveries so long eluded us?

We should recall in this connection that East Texas is equal in size, that is, in total content of recoverable hydrocarbons, to about 50 major American oilfields (a major oilfield is defined as one containing 100 million barrels or more of recoverable oil). Kuwait, in turn, is equal in size to a half dozen or more East Texas oilfields.

There are other puzzling episodes of a similar nature in the record of our search for oil over the earth. France, for example, over a period of many decades has starved for oil. For France to provide the foreign exchange required to pay for essential imports of oil from foreign sources — Venezuela and the Middle East — has for years posed a major financial problem. Yet France has long been recognized by geologists as a promising area in which to look for oilfields. And, indeed, within the past few years a number of fine oilfields have been found in France — several in the Paris Basin, next door to the capital city itself, and others in the Bordeaux Basin in the south of France. In French North Africa, too, recent exploration has discovered immense oil and gas fields. Why have these new prolific sources of oil gone for so long undetected in a nation which has so badly needed oil for so long? The French are excellent geologists — none better — trained and skilled in the art of oilfinding. It is not the art of prospecting that is at fault.

Now I have spoken glowingly of the achievement of oilfinders — their creation of an effective art of prospecting based on the science of geology — and I have asserted that the basic geologic principles of this art were announced — that is, they were published and became widely known to geologists in this country — soon after our first oilfield was discovered in 1859. Yet I must confess to you that our most generally available business histories reveal little evidence of these facts.

The American Petroleum Industry has recently published a magnificent history — sponsored by the API and edited by Harold F. Williamson, an eminent business historian. It is a splendid document covering the birth of the industry and its development up to 1900 — a volume of 800 pages with an exhaustive 30-page index.

Nowhere in this index, however, will you find the term "anticline," or "anticlinal theory"; nowhere in the text of this history will you find the name H. D. Rogers, of the Pennsylvania Geological Survey, who enunciated that theory in 1860; or the names of T. Sterry Hunt, or Sir Wm. Logan, who developed the same theory, independently, and published it in 1861. Only if you look in the appendix will you find the name of Israel C. White, popularly known as the "father of the anticlinal theory," who, in 1885, set himself up in West Virginia as a consulting geologist to apply this theory professionally to oilfinding.

You will find in this history the record of the tardy entry of the old Standard Oil group, late in the nineteenth century, into production and exploration for oil. But nowhere does the name of John Worthington, the colorful geologist who directed that exploration, appear. And nowhere is the fact revealed that the old Standard Oil firm, in its search for oil, also employed Israel C. White as a consulting geologist.

The new history does discuss for several pages the so-called "belt theory" of oil occurrence and the sensational feats of its inventor, an engineer named Angell, in locating "gushers" through its use. It discusses also the use of "dowsing," witching, telepathy, and clairvoyance in early attempts to find new oilfields. And it records the fact that early geologists disagreed about theories of origin and accumulation of oil, stirring up heated debates right here at Harvard almost as soon as Drake completed his first well. These early debates centered around that turbulent Swiss naturalist, Louis Agassiz, invariably critical of new scientific theory.

I shall not pursue further here my protest that current business history omits facts that to me are important. My comment is intended only to warn you that this API history does not support all the statements I make here. Explanations are easily at hand. The volume of new discoveries was of relatively small import until after the year 1900, the end of the period covered by this history. Our significant discoveries of new oilfields came later. Of our total discoveries of oil in this country to date, something like 99 per cent, quantitatively, came during the latter half of the life of the industry. Thus only 1 per cent of our discoveries were made during the period under review.

An even more potent cause of the omission of pioneer geological theory from the record historians have compiled of the early years of the American oil industry is the fact that the pertinent source material most readily available to historians consists largely of the files of newspapers published in the oil-producing regions at the time. It is inevitable that these newspapers, like newspapers generally, should have emphasized the sensational, dramatic events of the day — those touched with "human interest" — rather than the dry-as-dust transactions of geological societies.

But to return to the record of oilfinding: I have stated my conviction elsewhere that even the most finished art of prospecting, by itself, falls short of the needs of the oilfinder. Across his path loom obstacles that no mere perfection of techniques can surmount. To cope effectively with these barriers, the oilfinder must acquire a perspective which enables him to survey with comprehension a field much broader than mere technology. Oilfinding involves more than technology. Indeed, in some of its most significant aspects, oilfinding takes on the character of a psychological phenomenon. To elaborate this thesis would carry us far afield and I shall not impose such an excursion at this time. Perhaps I may epitomize, however, the conclusion at which I have inevitably arrived whenever

I have myself undertaken to explore this line of thought. That conclusion is: where new oilfields are really first discovered is in the minds of men.

If this is a sound conclusion, then it is the minds of men we should study if we would learn how oilfields are discovered, and if we would learn what may be equally valuable — how, upon occasion, great oilfields like East Texas and Kuwait, mysteriously escape discovery through years of vigorous exploration of the oil-producing region in which they are situated. To this end we should examine whatever record is available that will reveal the deliberations, as well as the actions, of the men who have directed exploration in the oil industry. What ideas governed their decisions to test — or to discard — the prospects that, one after another, were brought to their attention? Is it too much to hope that business history may come to provide the oilfinder with information of this character?

To illustrate the problem the oilfinder commonly faces, let us look at the available record of a significant oilfield discovery — Kuwait in the Middle East. As background it will be useful to review briefly the history of oil and gas in the region in which Kuwait is situated. We should note, first, that numerous conspicuous seepages of oil and gas at widely spaced places in the Middle East have attracted attention throughout historic time. References to these occurrences appear in the Bible. The discovery of commercial accumulations of petroleum in the Middle East came as no surprise, therefore, to leaders in the petroleum industry.

The British, whose government had long been dominant politically in the Middle East, were the first to undertake petroleum exploration there. Early in the nineteenth century Britain established virtual protectorates over the nominally independent sheikdoms around the Persian Gulf and during the first decades of the twentieth century she extended some of these treaties to obtain for herself a preferred position in the matter of possible concessions for the exploitation of petroleum resources.

In 1913, for example, Sheik Mabarak of Kuwait, who since 1898 had looked to Britain for protection against Turkey, gave to the British Political Resident in the Persian Gulf area a letter promising "to show the place of bitumen (oil seepages) at Burgan and elsewhere," and further assuring him "we shall never give a concession in this matter to anyone except a person appointed from the British

Government."[3] Burgan, the site of this reported seepage, is also, of course, the site of the present Kuwait oilfield.

Similarly, in 1914, the Sheik of Bahrein who, in 1880, had approved an "exclusive agreement" with Britain, wrote to the British Political Resident "if there is any prospect of obtaining kerosene oil in my territory of Bahrein, I will not embark on the exploitation of that myself and will not entertain overtures from any quarter regarding that without consulting the Political Agent in Bahrein and with the approval of the High Government."[4] In its geologic structure, Bahrein, an island near the head of the Persian Gulf, is a beautiful anticline on top of which a copious oil seepage has long been known. Both the anticline and the seepage were accurately described as early as 1908 by Dr. Pilgrim, a British geologist.

In 1901, a venturesome British merchant, William K. D'Arcy, secured a vast oil and gas concession in Persia. Distributed over the surface of this concession were great anticlines marked by oil and gas seepages.

In 1907, D'Arcy made his first significant discovery on one of these anticlines, and by 1914 Persia had already become an important oil-producing nation. At the outbreak of the First World War the British House of Commons, under the influence of Winston Churchill, authorized the purchase by the British Admiralty of a controlling interest in D'Arcy's thriving enterprise, which was thenceforth called the Anglo-Persian Oil Company.

American oil interests first attempted to gain a foothold in the Middle East immediately after the close of the First World War. In 1928, following a long period of negotiation, two American companies, Jersey Standard Oil and Socony Vacuum, finally secured small minority participation in Iraq Petroleum Company, an international group, dominated by Anglo-Persian Oil but including, in addition to the Americans, the French government and the Royal Dutch Shell. In 1927, even before its corporate organization had been finally achieved in 1928, Iraq Petroleum Company completed an oil well which discovered one of the world's half-dozen largest oilfields on a magnificent anticline at Kirkuk in Iraq. With the discovery at Kirkuk, the historic oil seepages (bitumen) in Kuwait took on added significance; an oil-producing country now flanked it on either side — to the east in Persia, and to the west in Iraq.

[3] India, Foreign Department. A Collection of Treaties, 1928, pp. 264–265, quoted by Frederick Lee Moore, Jr., "A Thesis presented to the School of Politics and International Affairs, Princeton University, 1948."
[4] India, A Collection of Treaties, p. 239.

As has repeatedly been the case in the discovery of great oil-fields, the first definite plan to explore for oil in Kuwait must be credited to a soldier of fortune with something of the character of the promoter. Late in the year 1920 a New Zealander, Major Frank Holmes, a mining engineer and a familiar figure in the Middle East, opened negotiations for petroleum concessions more or less simultaneously with the sheiks of Bahrein and Kuwait and the king of Saudi Arabia. Major Holmes was an impressive figure — burly, loquacious, picturesque — with a gift for showmanship. His manner of approach to the local rulers was spectacular and persuasive, and within a short time all his negotiations succeeded.

Meantime, early in the 1920's, Major Holmes had already opened a vigorous campaign to dispose of the concessions he hoped to obtain. He went first to London and, naturally enough, to the Anglo-Persian, the company best qualified by experience and knowledge to appraise realistically the potentialities of the concessions he offered for sale. When he failed with Anglo-Persian he went next to Royal Dutch Shell and when again he failed to make a sale, he came to New York and to Jersey Standard Oil. But Jersey, like its two great international competitors, also refused Major Holmes' offer. And so these three leading oil companies each permitted the chance to acquire the Kuwait oilfield to slip through their fingers.

Despite his failure to interest either of the three companies who were his most likely customers, Major Holmes and an associate, Thomas E. Ward, persisted in their sales effort on both sides of the Atlantic. All through the early and middle 1920's these two haunted the offices of the big oil companies both in London and New York. At length, toward the end of November, 1927, Ward succeeded in selling to Gulf Oil Corporation, a company which had been up to that time a practical stranger to the Middle East, a concession covering Kuwait and Bahrein, together with a tenuous claim (which Gulf failed to validate) to a part of Saudi Arabia.

The terms of the concession Gulf had acquired from Major Holmes specified prompt drilling of an exploratory well. In order to meet this obligation, Gulf assigned to another total stranger to the Middle East — Standard Oil Company of California — the concession on Bahrein on condition that this company drill the required test. A considerable delay ensued before the British government saw fit to approve the entry of the California company into Bahrein. But eventually this approval was secured and in October, 1931, drilling began on the test well, located on the oil seepage near the center of the island. It was completed — a flowing well — in June, 1932, discovering the Bahrein oilfield.

With an oil well on Bahrein, Gulf's Kuwait concession on the adjacent mainland suddenly became very attractive. This concession also required the approval of Great Britain, by reason of its long-standing "Exclusive Agreement" with Kuwait. This approval was not obtained until 1935, after the Gulf had transferred a one-half interest in the Kuwait prospect to the British-controlled Anglo-Iranian Oil Company (formerly Anglo-Persian Oil Company, now British Petroleum Company). With this concession a new, jointly owned Kuwait Oil Company, Ltd., was chartered and a new concession negotiated. It was not until May, 1938, that Kuwait Oil Company, Ltd., completed the discovery well in what was to become the world's greatest oilfield near the seepage at Burgan, Kuwait.

Here, then, is a bare outline of the available data on the discovery of the Kuwait oilfield. In it we encounter a curious incident in the record of our search for oil. For years a diligent broker goes about the world striving vainly to sell to the leading units in the industry the greatest of all our oilfields. For years he finds no buyer. Did our most enlightened oilfinding enterprises fail to recognize the true nature of the prospect which concealed the greatest oilfield we have ever known? Surely the art of prospecting was adequate to the task of identifying Kuwait as a likely prospect. Why, then, was this great prize allowed to fall into the lap of a relative stranger to the oil industry in the Middle East? Even more tantalizing is the query: What induced Gulf to venture into an enterprise which, to its better informed competitors, appeared to offer so little possible reward?

It is not that complicated geologic structure obscured the promise of oil accumulation at Kuwait. The surface evidences alone were persuasive. It is not that the price asked by Major Holmes was excessive. The concessions were offered for a song — a cash payment of a paltry $50,000 plus an obligation to drill a single exploratory well. It is not that the concessions lay in unpromising territory, or in a region unknown to the oil industry. The phenomenal oilfields of Persia, adjacent to Kuwait on the east, had already been producing for three decades before the Kuwait concession was finally proved. And the multi-billion-barrel Kirkuk field in Iraq, just west of Kuwait, had been discovered before Major Holmes finally made his sale. The companies that refused the offer of

Kuwait were already engaged in producing oil nearby. They were familiar with this greatest of our petroleum provinces.

This episode plagues the student of oilfinding. With him a prime objective is to learn what it is that leads to the discovery of oilfields. But he seeks, also, to learn what it is that stands in the way of these same discoveries. "History," it is said, "presents the story not only of man's achievements, but also of his failures." [5] The oilfinder needs business histories of oil companies operating in the Middle East that present the story, not only of their achievements in discovering new oilfields there, but also of their failures.

Several Middle East oil companies have published business histories. Some of these mention the discovery of Kuwait. But I have failed to find any published account of the facts adequate to the oilfinder's needs. The records of both the venture that succeeds and the venture that fails to discover a new oilfield are essential to the art of oilfinding. It may be urged that the institutions which teach the earth science should include in their courses of instruction case histories of the discoveries of outstanding oilfields. But where is the academician to turn for the facts? Too often these are buried in the confidential files of oil companies. I would like to believe that histories of companies engaged in the search for oil will eventually supply this data.

Unfortunately, of course, a serious lag usually intervenes between the development of new knowledge by industry and the incorporation of that knowledge into our textbooks. Moreover, business history, at best, can never be brought quite up to date. But is it unreasonable to ask that the duration of this inevitable hiatus be reduced to a minimum — reduced to a single decade, say, from the existing two decades or more?

If business history is to serve the oilfinder effectively it must provide him with a full, reasonably up-to-date record of collective experience in oilfinding. I am reminded of a sentiment carried recently on the masthead of a British industrial journal: "Every business firm has an obligation to the contemporary historian to have its history written and an obligation to the future historian to preserve certain of its current records." [6] This is a sentiment which I, as an oilfinder, wish heartily to applaud. The "current records" which the oilfinding profession needs from business history include a candid record of the decisions taken by the major units engaged in

---

[5] Richard E. Weaver, University of Chicago. The Intercollegiate Society of Individualists, Inc. *Wall Street Journal* (Oct. 9, 1959).

[6] *The Manager, Journal of the British Institute of Management* (April, 1959), p. 240.

the search for oil — a record of their failures as well as their successes.

"A knowledge of history," Carl Becker has observed, "serves the individual, not because it enables him to predict the future but because it enables him to anticipate and thus to meet the future." [7] Adequate business histories of corporations which engage in the search for oil should enable the men and women who guide that search better to meet the future demands for new oilfields.

[7] Carl Becker, *Modern History* (1935), p. vi.

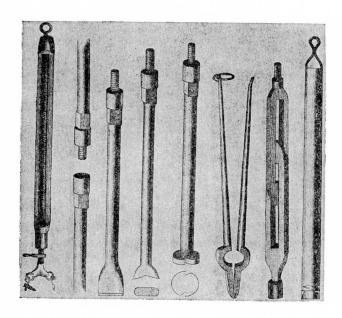

Competitive Structure of the

American Petroleum Industry
1880-1911

A Reappraisal

by Harold F. Williamson and
Ralph L. Andreano

NORTHWESTERN UNIVERSITY

It is quite commonly assumed, even among certain scholars, that for some 30 years prior to 1911 Standard Oil's dominant position in the American Petroleum Industry was virtually unchallenged.[1] A close examination of the data covering the history of the industry during this period, however, strongly suggests that changes in the structure of the industry through the entry of new firms after 1911

[1] Joel Dirlam, for example, author of the chapter, "The Petroleum Industry," in *The Structure of American Industry*, Walter B. Adams, ed. (New York, 1954), pp. 236–237, says: "From 1883, when the Standard Oil Company acquired the last independent pipeline of importance, to 1911 when it was dissolved under the anti-trust laws, Standard bought, transported, refined, and marketed some 90% of U. S. petroleum."

TABLE I

U. S. Crude Oil Production, by Major Fields: 1874–1911
(*In millions of 42-gallon barrels*)

	Appalachian	Lima-Indiana	Gulf Coast	California	Mid-Continent	Illinois	All Other	Total
1874								
No. of barrels	10.9	..	..	..	..	..	..	10.9
Percentage of total production	100	..	..	..	..	..	..	100
1879								
No. of barrels	19.8	..	..	..	..	..	.1	19.9
Percentage of total production	100	..	..	..	..	..	a	100
1884								
No. of barrels	23.9	..	..	..	..	..	.3	24.2
Percentage of total production	99	..	..	..	..	..	1	100
1889								
No. of barrels	22.3	12.2	..	..	..	..	.7	35.2
Percentage of total production	63	35	..	..	..	..	2	100
1894								
No. of barrels	30.8	17.3	..	..	..	..	1.2	49.3
Percentage of total production	63	35	..	..	..	..	2	100
1899								
No. of barrels	33.0	20.2	..	2.6	..	..	1.3	57.1
Percentage of total production	58	35	..	5	..	..	2	100
1901								
No. of barrels	33.6	21.9	3.6	8.8	1.0	..	.6	69.5
Percentage of total production	48	32	5	13	1	..	1	100
1903								
No. of barrels	31.5	24.0	18.4	24.4	1.6	..	.6	100.5
Percentage of total production	31	24	18	24	2	..	1	100
1905								
No. of barrels	29.4	22.3	36.5	33.4	12.5	.2	.4	134.7
Percentage of total production	22	16	27	25	9	a	a	100
1907								
No. of barrels	25.3	10.0	15.8	44.9	46.9	24.3	..	167.2
Percentage of total production	15	6	9	27	28	15	..	100
1909								
No. of barrels	26.5	8.2	9.7	55.5	50.8	30.9	1.6	183.2
Percentage of total production	14	4	5	30	28	17	2	100
1911								
No. of barrels	23.7	6.2	11.0	81.1	66.6	31.3	.5	220.4
Percentage of total production	11	3	5	37	30	14	a	100

a Less than 1 per cent.
SOURCE: Basic data from Ralph Arnold and William Kemnitzer, *Petroleum in the U. S. and Possessions* (New York, 1931), p. 33.

were essentially a projection of a trend already well advanced at the time of the formal dissolution of the Standard Oil Company.[2]

Quite aside from any deterioration in Standard's market position attributable to general economic growth, the circumstances leading to new entrants into the industry may be grouped under three main headings: [3]

1. A growth in the number and location of new flush fields that, because of minimal barriers to entry posed by absolute capital requirements and economies of scale, enabled established firms to expand and new firms to obtain crude supplies necessary to begin operations.

2. The quality and quantity of crude oil discoveries, which played an important role in types of products produced and sold and, in turn, facilitated the process of entry via effects on market segmentation.

3. Incorrect, or insufficiently rapid, market response on the part of the dominant firm (Standard Oil) which left market opportunities, or market space, not only for the exploitation of crude deposits but also for the distribution of "old" and "new" products.

Changes in Standard Oil's relative position in the industry between 1880 and 1911 are summarized in Table II. In respect to crude oil, for example, Standard maintained its predominant control over production in the Appalachian, Lima-Indiana, and Illinois fields between 1880 and 1911. But the proportion of crude from California, Mid-Continent, and Gulf Coast fields going to independents had by 1911 reduced Standard's share of total domestic production during this period from over 90 per cent to approximately 60–65 per cent. This decline in the company's relative share of domestic crude production was closely matched by a decrease in the proportion of total refining capacity under Standard's control from approximately 90–95 per cent in 1880 to 60–65 per cent in 1911. The impact of these shifts on Standard's general marketing position was varied. By 1911, however, the independents were supplying nearly 70 per cent of the fuel oil; some 45 per cent of the lubricants; a third of the gasoline and waxes; and about one quarter of the kerosene distributed by the American Petroleum Industry.

These changes, coupled with the emergence of a dozen or more integrated concerns plus a large number of smaller companies

[2] Source materials for this article were: Harold F. Williamson and Arnold R. Daum, *A History of the American Petroleum Industry, 1859–1900: The Age of Illumination* (Evanston, Ill., 1959); Ralph and Muriel Hidy, *Pioneering in Big Business: History of Standard Oil Company (New Jersey)*, vol. I (New York, 1955); Ralph L. Andreano, "The Emergence of New Competition in the American Petroleum Industry Before 1911" (unpublished doctoral thesis, Northwestern University, Evanston, Ill., 1960).

[3] Some indication of the magnitude and relative importance of crude production by major fields is given in Table I.

specializing in one or more phases of the oil business, suggest a competitive structure in 1911 that was a far cry from the late 1870's, when Standard Oil and the American Petroleum Industry were practically synonymous.

TABLE II

SUMMARY OF STANDARD OIL'S POSITION IN THE AMERICAN PETROLEUM INDUSTRY 1880–1911

PERCENTAGE CONTROL OVER CRUDE OIL SUPPLIES				
Fields	1880	1899	1906	1911
Appalachian [a]	92	88	72	78
Lima-Indiana	..	85	95	90
Gulf Coast [b]	..	..	10	10
Mid-Continent [c]	..	..	45	44
Illinois [d]	..	..	100	83
California [e]	..	..	29	29

PERCENTAGE CONTROL OVER REFINERY CAPACITY				
	1880	1899	1906	1911
Share of Rated Daily Crude Capacity	90–95	82	70	64

PERCENTAGE OF MAJOR PRODUCTS SOLD [f]			
	1880	1899	1906 – 1911 [g]
Kerosene	90–95	85	75
Lubes	..	40	55
Waxes	..	50	67
Fuel Oil [h]	..	85	31
Gasoline	..	85	66

[a] Share of pipeline runs. Does not include sales of crude by Standard to independents. If these are included, Standard's share of Appalachian crude should read: 1899, 80%; 1906, 40%; 1911, 50%. Approximately 2% of Standard's Lima-Indiana runs were sold to independents.

[b] Standard had no pipeline connection in the original Gulf fields; it was a relatively passive buyer of crude. In 1909 Standard had a trunk line connection from Mid-Continent through Louisiana; but this was to tap Mid-Continent crude rather than Gulf-Louisiana crude. Above figures are Standard Oil consumption of Gulf crude.

[c] Figures refer to Prairie Oil & Gas Company share of Mid-Continent crude available for shipment to consumption points.

[d] Ohio Oil Company pipeline runs as per cent of total field production.

[e] Standard did not formally enter California in an integrated way until 1900 when it acquired Pacific Coast Oil Company.

[f] These are all rough estimates.

[g] Figures available only for 1906 and 1910 from Standard; 1908 for other firms. Because of this, both the lube and wax estimates may be overstated. In general, however, for somewhere in the middle of the 1906–1911 period the above figures are a close approximation of relative market shares in the respective products.

[h] Includes residual fuel oil and unrefined crude sold as fuel.

SOURCE: Andreano, "The Emergence of New Competition in the American Petroleum Industry Before 1911."

The circumstances and processes by which new companies entered the industry during the period before 1911 may be illustrated by reference to developments associated with the emergence of the major new crude producing areas.

APPALACHIAN

Standard Oil's position in the American industry late in the 1870's was based essentially on ownership (or lease) of some 90 per cent of domestic refining capacity, plus virtually a monopoly control of facilities for gathering and transporting crude oil. But even Standard found it impossible between 1876 and 1882 to expand its gathering lines, storage, and transport facilities rapidly enough to accommodate an approximate trebling of output of crude — largely from Bradford, the first modern flush field, in the Appalachian oil regions.

The result was a sufficient supply of crude outside Standard's control to provide the basis for the emergence of two types of firms: (1) fully integrated companies producing a complete line of refinery products, such as the Tidewater Oil Company and a group that was subsequently merged to form the Pure Oil Company, and (2) companies (partially or fully integrated), including the Union Petroleum Company, Crew-Levick, and the Pennzoil Company, that specialized in the production of lubricating oils and wax.

The immediate impact of Bradford on Standard's position in the industry is reflected in the Trust's share of total refining capacity, which fell from about 90 per cent in the late 1870's to approximately 75 per cent by 1884. Some of this loss was subsequently regained and for the entire 1880–1899 period Standard's share of total refining capacity declined about 10 per cent; its share of Appalachian crude production over the same period dropped from 92 to 88 per cent. The most important effect of Bradford (supplemented by the growth of production in Lima-Indiana), however, was in the reduction of Standard's share of the production of lubricants and waxes from 75 per cent or more in 1880 to approximately 40 per cent of lubricants and 50 per cent of waxes by 1899.

LIMA-INDIANA

Production that began to expand in the Lima-Indiana fields in the mid-1880's, and reached a peak in 1896, prompted Standard Oil to move quickly into the area with an extensive system of gathering lines, storage facilities, and crude trunk lines. Even so,

Standard's control over output that, measured by pipeline runs, was approximately 93 per cent in 1894, declined to about 85 per cent by 1899.

Chiefly because of the quality of the crude (sold largely as fuel oil until the development by Standard of the Frasch process) and the costs of entry, Standard Oil was the only established company to move into the Lima-Indiana fields.

The Lima-Indiana fields did, however, provide an opportunity for new entrants, including the Sun Oil Company, the National Refining Company, and the Paragon Oil Company. Moreover, these companies were fully integrated, with their own production, pipelines, and refining and marketing facilities. While fuel oil was their major product, by adopting refining techniques similar to the Frasch process, all were producing a full product line by 1899.

While the independents' share of the market was relatively modest — probably no more than 15 per cent in respect to fuel oil and much less in other products — the experience gained in exploiting the industrial demand for petroleum fuel oil was an important factor in subsequent decisions to move into the Gulf area after the turn of the century.[4]

GULFCOAST

In contrast to Lima-Indiana, Standard Oil did not formally enter the Gulf Coast region, where crude production reached its peak about 1905. Three reasons have generally been cited in explaining this response on the part of Standard: (1) the legal climate in Texas — where an antitrust action had been instituted against the Waters-Pierce Company, Standard's major marketing affiliate in the state; (2) the refining quality of the Texas crude, which yielded relatively small amounts of kerosene, the product that Standard was primarily interested in refining and; (3) the feeling on the part of Standard officials that Mid-Continent and California offered better investment opportunities than Gulf, both in respect to the quantity and quality of crudes needed for their operations. Standard's role in the Gulf Coast development was thus limited to the purchase of an estimated 10 per cent of the output from the region.

With some 90 per cent of Gulf Coast crude output available for

---

[4] Production of crude in Ohio and Indiana also had repercussions on the organization of the eastern segment of the industry that may be labeled the "Lima-effect." In brief, the process may be described as follows: (1) crude from the Lima fields could only be refined to produce fuel oil and kerosene; (2) firms making lubricants and wax from Appalachian crude — which yielded more desirable (in terms of market acceptance) qualities of lubricants and wax, changed their product mix to maximize outputs of these products, rather than kerosene; (3) the effect was to increase the proportion of these products supplied by eastern firms relative to Standard Oil which was committed to processing Lima crude.

"outsiders," the impact on the structure of the industry — and on Standard's position — was quite significant. Of the already established firms in the Appalachian and Lima-Indiana regions, Sun Oil Company moved most rapidly to use Gulf crude as a springboard for a highly successful program of expansion that made the company one of the leading factors in the industry, particularly in the production and distribution of fuel oil and lubricants. Pure Oil was also able to acquire a modest interest in the Gulf fields.

The most significant structural changes stimulated by Gulf Coast developments, however, were attributable to *de novo* entrants into the industry. These were of two types. First, there were fully integrated companies such as Gulf Oil Company and the Texas Company that attempted to produce a full product line but were more successful for several years as distributors of fuel oil. Second, there were the fuel oil companies, about 20 in all, that did not operate refineries (because the crude oil could be sold as fuel after exposure to the sun had evaporated the light ends), but were integrated from production to marketing facilities.

As a result of these developments in the Gulf region, Standard Oil, for the first time since the mid-1880's, did not "establish" crude prices in the United States. Moreover, with the expansion of the established firms and the addition of the new entrants drawing their crude from the Gulf fields, oligopoly behavior — a characteristic commonly associated with the present-day petroleum industry — became distinctly recognizable. This was particularly true in respect to the fuel oil market, where less than a dozen firms accounted for the great bulk of sales. The increasing importance of independents in the expanding fuel market was further reflected by a decline in Standard's relative market share from about 85 per cent in 1899 to 31 per cent in 1906–1911.

MID-CONTINENT

Mid-Continent provided the basis for an even more significant expansion of established independents and the entry of new firms in the industry. Not only did the strike at Glenn Pool in 1905 establish the region as a major producing area in the United States, but the crude was an Appalachian type that yielded relatively large proportions of gasoline and kerosene as well as high quality lube stocks.

Standard Oil understandably was quick to acquire leases and to build gathering lines, storage facilities, and trunk pipelines in Mid-

Continent. But other companies were also quick to move into Mid-Continent. Among the leaders were the firms already operating in the Gulf region, notably Gulf Oil and the Texas Company; National Petroleum and Sun Oil, that had started in Lima-Indiana; the Associated Oil Company, a California concern; the Union Petroleum Company; Crew-Levick; and Pure Oil and Tidewater, pioneer processors of Appalachian crudes. In addition, the Mid-Continent provided the basis for the emergence of almost a score of partially or fully integrated firms, listed in Table III.

TABLE III

SIZE CHARACTERISTICS OF OKLAHOMA-KANSAS INDEPENDENTS, 1906–1911

Name of Firm	Crude Production	Daily Crude Oil Capacity of Refineries (in 42-gallon barrels)	Pipeline Mileage (miles)	No. of R.R. Tankers	No. of Distribution Stations
American Refining Co.[a][b][c]		1500	[c]	[c]	[c]
Chanute Refining Co.[d]	Yes	1750	60	290	33
Cudahy Refining Co.[a][d]	Yes	6000	128	335	610
Great Western Refining Co.[a]	Yes	2000	24	40	1
Indiahoma Refining Co.	Yes	1200	43	83	3
Kansas City Refining Co.[a]	No	1000	[c]	42	[c]
Kansas Oil Refining Co. [c]		1800	60	52	[c]
Kansas Co-operative Refining Co.[a]	Yes	500	6	30	20
Kanotex Refining Co.[f]	Yes	1000	33	41	31
Milliken Refining Co.[a][d] [c]		4000	65	370	[c]
Muskogee Refining Co.[a][b]	Yes	1440	18	49	8
National Refining Co.[a][g]	Yes	3000	110	315	50[h]
Oklahoma Refining Co.[b] [c]		600	7	40	50
Petroleum Producing Co.[a]	Yes	3500	170	182	[c]
Paola Refining Co.[i][b]	Yes	(150)[i]	40	[c]	[c]
Sapulpa Refining Co.	No	3000	35	69	[c]
Uncle Sam Oil Co.	Yes	1400	[c]	88	7

[a] Also had separate lube oil plants.
[b] Merged into Cities Service Corp.
[c] Not available.
[d] Became part of Sinclair Oil Co.
[e] Used Mid-Continent crude by tank cars; sold all its refined output, including considerable fuel oil, to jobbers in Kansas City, Missouri, area.
[f] Now property of Anderson-Prichard Oil Co.
[g] Absorbed by Ashland Oil & Refining Co.
[h] Does not include operations in East.
[i] Taken over in 1907 by Standard Asphalt and Rubber Co. Standard continued to operate the petroleum refinery, and by end of 1911 had expanded daily crude capacity to about 2000 barrels. The asphalt plant had another 1000 barrels per day crude capacity. Standard was an extremely successful manufacturer of roofing and paving material, marketing its products under the brand name "Sarco." In 1917, J. Ogden Armour, who then owned Standard Asphalt, sold all his holdings to Cities Service.

SOURCE: Andreano, "The Emergence of New Competition in the American Petroleum Industry Before 1911."

With Standard's control over Mid-Continent crude production limited to about 45 per cent during 1905–1911, the effect of the growth of independents was to extend competition beyond the fuel oil market into the sale and distribution of kerosene, gasoline, and lubricants. The extent to which The Texas Company, for example, had diversified its product line by 1907 is indicated in Table IV, a listing which also provides a reasonably complete checklist of petroleum products of the day. The results of this expansion were most noticeable in the reduction between 1899 and 1906–1911 of Standard's share of kerosene distribution from about 85 per cent to 75 per cent, and of gasoline from about 85 per cent to approximately 66 per cent.

TABLE IV

Texaco Product Line, November, 1907

ILLUMINATING OILS

Homelight Oil	Guaranteed to be the equal of any and superior to most of the kerosenes on the market. No smoke and no odor. A perfect illuminant.
Crystal Oil	A low-priced, perfectly safe and satisfactory illuminant.

GASOLINES AND NAPHTHAS

Deodorized and High-Test Gasoline	For gas machines, soldering machines, racing automobiles, auto-boats, etc.
Deodorized Stove Gasoline	For gasoline stoves, automobiles, gasoline engines, dry cleaning, torches, etc.
Deodorized Engine Naphtha	For gasoline engines, automobiles, launches.
Varnish Makers' and Paint Makers' Naphtha	For mixing paints.
Texene	A perfect substitute for turpentine in mixing paints, varnish, etc., and sold at a lower price.

LUBRICATING OILS

No. 1 Texaco Engine Oil	A light pale oil, suitable for high-speed engines, dynamos, spindles, and all bearings requiring a light and free-running lubricant.
No. 2 Texaco Engine Oil	A superior high viscosity pale oil especially adapted to engine and dynamo work.
No. 3 Texaco Engine Oil	Our highest grade engine oil, bright red with a greenish cast, recommended for the most rigorous service, such as marine engines, turbines, etc.

SOURCE: These are extracts from a pamphlet "Petroleum and Its Products" issued by The Texas Co. in connection with its exhibit at a Dallas fair in 1907. Reprinted in *Oil Investor's Journal* (Nov. 5, 1907), pp. 20–21.

No. 4 Texaco
Engine Oil

A general purpose red oil. It will give satisfaction.

Texaco Ammonia Oil

An oil of exceptionally low cold text with superior lubricating qualities.

CYLINDER STOCKS

No. 1 Texaco
Cylinder Oil

A highly filtered perfect valve lubricant.

No. 2 Texaco
Cylinder Oil

A filtered oil of high lubricating value.

No. 3 Texaco
Cylinder Oil

As good an oil as we or anyone else can make.

No. 4 Texaco
Cylinder Oil

An oil of exceptionally high fire test, adapted to marine and other high-pressure engines.

No. 5 Texaco
Cylinder Oil

A general purpose valve oil low in price, high in quality.

No. 6 Texaco
Cylinder Oil

Especially suited to use in machines, it has superior filtering qualities.

SPECIAL LUBRICANTS

Texaco Gas
Engine Oil

A combination oil for gas engine cylinders and bearings.

Texaco Automobile
Oil

An oil that does not carbonize, but does lubricate automobile cylinders.

No. 1 Texaco Castor
Machine Oil

For harvesters, journals, and fast-running machinery. Extra heavy in body.

Texaco Harvester
Oil

For harvesters, planers, axles, etc.

Texaco Journal Oil

A heavy, dark green oil, guaranteed satisfactory for general work such as shafting, crushers, harvesters, windmills, and all agricultural machinery.

Texaco Winter
Black

A good, cheap lubricant for outdoor work. It will not congeal in cold weather. A good car oil.

Texaco Curve
Oil

An oil adapted especially for street car use, oiling curves, etc.

Texaco Threadcutting
Oil

A most efficient and economical product.

Texaco Saw Oil

For preventing the gumming of saws when cutting resinous woods.

OTHER PRODUCTS

Texaco Cattle
Dipping Oil

A crude petroleum prepared according to a formula adopted and recommended by the Bureau of Animal Industry, U. S. Dept. of Agriculture, for the extermination of ticks, lice, and other vermin and the cure of mange in cattle hogs.

Texaco Road Oil	With this commodity the renowned oil roads of California can be duplicated, and constructed and maintained, at less than half the cost of macadam.
Fuel Oil	The superiority of fuel oil over coal is universally recognized. The Texas Co. is the largest distributor of this commodity in the Southwest.
Texaco Asphalts	Over 99% pure bitumen.
Texaco Paving Cement	A sheet asphalt pavement made of Texaco asphalt has pre-eminently the following properties:

First — It will not crush or grind away at any climatic temperature by reason of its pliability and elasticity at all temperatures.

Second — Being ductile even at the lowest temperatures obtained, the pavement may contract without cracking.

Third — It possesses the necessary firmness at the maximum climatic temperature obtained to withstand the passage of traffic without being cut into so badly as to be objectionable or put to the side of the street. At the same time it will maintain a rubbery, noiseless surface.

Fourth — Its density precludes the entrance of water and it does not contain any material that is acted upon by water.

Fifth — It will not age so rapidly as to cause the pavement to lose its pliability before a reasonable time.

Sixth — Texaco paving cements do not require fluxing.

Special grades are reprepared for paving brick filler and sanitary mastic floors.

Texaco Roofing Cements	Texaco roofing cements are made in four grades with melting points and consistencies to meet all conditions of climate, being absolutely impervious to water, tenacious, pliable and durable at all temperatures.
Texaco Water-Proofing Cements	Absolutely impervious to water. Manufactured expressly for water-proofing underground concrete and brick construction, and for lining in water reservoirs. Texaco water-proofing cements are very adhesive and give perfect protection to underground iron and steel work and can be applied with equally good results to wooden construction, and will not crack or disintegrate.
Texaco Mineral Rubber Pipe Dip	A high-melting point product, especially efficient in protecting metal pipes from the injurious effects of chemicals in soil and water. It is tough and adhesive and will not crack or peel when properly applied.

COMPETITIVE STRUCTURE IN THE INDUSTRY   81

Texaco Mineral Rubber Insulating Cement	Used in packing houses, cold storage plants and by manufacturers of electrical materials and appliances, where perfect insulation and damp-proofing is required.
Texaco Tank Bottom Cement	Used to protect the bottom of steel tanks inside and out.
Texaco Asphalt Paint	A high-grade protection coating for metal surfaces.
Texaco Liquid Asphalt	An unequaled flux for natural asphalts. It is free from volatile oils and coke and of highest flash and fire test. It is considered the "standard."
Texaco Felt Roofing	Texaco felt roofing is manufactured according to a process developed and used exclusively by The Texas Co. and embodies qualities and characteristics which, we believe, render it more durable and satisfactory from every standpoint, than any other roofing now on the market.

Texaco felt roofing is sold in three weights — No. 1, No. 2, and No. 3 — thoroughly saturated, plied and coated with Texaco asphalt, which has a melting point of 220° F. and a fire test of 600° F., making it impervious to the sun and action of the elements, as well as being a protection from fire. The No. 1 weight is an all wool felt, and weighs about 41 pounds per square, while No. 2 and No. 3 are made from two layers of the same grade, weighing about 56 and 62 pounds per square, respectively.

Texaco felt roofing has no "top" or "bottom," being coated with Texaco asphalt as thoroughly on one side as on the other, giving protection underneath as well as on the top. Many instances are known where gases in certain manufacturing plants destroy roofing from underneath.

Texaco asphalt entering into the composition of Texaco felt roofing is refined to a degree rendering the roofing perfectly pliable and practically nonexpanding and not affected by heat or cold. It never hardens or becomes brittle and breaks up as in the case of many other roofings.

Texaco felt roofing costs no more and is guaranteed to last longer than any other roofing on the market. It is cheaper and better than tin, slate, or shingles. Samples will be sent on application.

ILLINOIS

Standard's relative position in the industry would no doubt have deteriorated even more by 1906–1911 if the organization had not succeeded in controlling some 85 per cent of the Appalachian type crude produced in the Illinois fields, which reached their peak during 1907–1911. Yet the remaining 15 per cent of the Illinois output was sufficient to make it worthwhile for Tidewater to acquire production in the area and extend its trunk pipeline from Pennsylvania to southeastern Illinois, as well as to enable the Indian Refining Company (later absorbed by The Texas Company) to emerge by 1911 as a fully integrated concern.

CALIFORNIA

In many respects the structure of the petroleum industry in California to 1911 followed a pattern of development that was radically different from the evolution of the industry east of the Rockies. It is true that by extending its marketing organization into California during the 1880's, Standard Oil remained the dominant distributor of kerosene on the West Coast until 1911. But the asphaltic based California crude, ill-suited for the production of kerosene or lube stocks, had little attraction for Standard, which did not acquire any producing properties, pipelines, or refineries in California until 1900. By that date, however, production in California (which by 1906 was as important quantitatively as output from Mid-Continent) was already split more or less equally among some seven integrated companies engaged primarily in the production and distribution of fuel oil.[5] Thus for a decade or more prior to 1911, the California industry had virtually all the characteristics of an oligopoly.[6]

CONCLUSION

If, as suggested by the foregoing material, the American Petroleum Industry was significantly influenced by the characteristics associated with new flush fields, it would seem that some revision is necessary in appraising the emergence of the modern structure of the industry. In other words, it appears that the basic forces generally recognized as stimulating the entry and expansion of vertically integrated firms during the 1920's were also operating in the 30-year period prior to 1911.

Similarly, it may be instructive to reinterpret the conservation

[5] In addition to Standard of California, these included the Union Oil Company, Associated Oil Company, Kern Trading & Oil Company, General Petroleum Company, Independent Oil Producers' Agency, and the Santa Fe Railroad.

[6] Mention should be made of the participation by the major California oil companies along with a dozen or more smaller concerns in the production and distribution of asphalt.

and prorationing movement in terms of what historically was the most common route for new firms to enter the industry. There are, of course, other important barriers to entry besides access to crude oil, notably product differentiation, economies of scale in refining, and aggregate capital requirements. Yet it can be argued that the effect of prorationing, introduced early in the 1930's, was a major factor in freezing the competitive structure of the petroleum industry; that the driving competitive forces formerly unleashed by flush field developments became a thing of the past.

If it is desirable to have more firms of more nearly equal size competing under reasonably similar structural conditions, a policy favoring free access to crude supplies via the flush field mechanism would appear to have considerable merit from the national standpoint. It may well be that the social-welfare gains through conservation and prorationing more than offset any advantages that might be realized through a policy that would allow flush field developments. The prorationing and conservation movement should, however, be re-examined in strictly economic, as well as social and political terms, and it is clear that flush fields played a more positive contributory role than hitherto assumed in the historical development of the industry's structure.

LOWERING THE CARTRIDGE

A
Case Study
of
Pricing Patterns

by Edmund P. Learned

HARVARD BUSINESS SCHOOL

Gentlemen, it is a privilege to speak to this group today on a forthcoming book on *Gasoline Pricing in Ohio* which Miss Catherine C. Ellsworth and I have prepared.[1] First, let me warn you that you are faced with a decided change in pace and may wonder how this topic, which involves a microscopic analysis of pricing practices and pricing data in one state for a period of 20 years, 1937–1957, fits in the 100-year history of the petroleum industry in the United States.

Other papers have dealt with various functional aspects of the 100-year history of the oil industry, and references have been made

[1] Edmund P. Learned and Catherine C. Ellsworth, *Gasoline Pricing in Ohio*, Division of Research, Harvard Business School (Boston, 1959). Reproduced through courtesy of the Division of Research.

to the Standard Oil Trust, how it came about, and why it was broken up. As historians well know, the Standard Oil Trust was alleged to have monopoly price objectives as a part of its strategy. There is no question that price leadership in one of its several forms developed in the field of gasoline pricing and that after the dissolution of the trust into regional Standard Oil companies price leadership was exercised by many of them. Unsophisticated persons, even as late as the 1920's, may have assumed that monopoly pricing of gasoline was the outstanding characteristic of the oil industry. Oil companies, on the other hand, who operated during the 1930's, 1940's (barring the war years when prices were controlled), and 1950's are prompt to state that these conceptions were not applicable during these periods and that the economic and competitive realities were quite different. Our research study brings facts to bear on such questions.

I first investigated the price leadership practices of The Standard Oil Company (Ohio) in 1937–1938 because the company, like many other oil companies, had been charged with monopolistic practices in connection with an antitrust suit, later dismissed without trial. The management wanted an outsider to investigate its facts and practices and let the chips fall where they might. The results of this study were published in the *Harvard Business Review* (November, 1948). Two of my colleagues, who are well-recognized economists, urged further investigation to bring the old study up to date, and fuller publication of the many facts available. Data collection began in 1954. Miss Ellsworth joined me in field research in 1955. Our results will be published on December 14, 1959.

It is not possible in the time allotted to give much more than a flavor of what the book is all about. The following summary is designed to give some feel for this particular research study. We hope it will have a place in the historical literature of the industry.

❖ ❖ ❖

This study of price leadership and competition in the retail and tank wagon markets of Ohio, which is focused mainly but not wholly on the period 1950–1955, is built around the following major research questions: (1) What pricing policies and practices have been evolved by the leading gasoline supplier in Ohio, and how far is this leader free to determine the prices at which it will sell at either the retail or tank wagon levels? (2) How prevalent are local price adjustments, and what factors influence the price leader to sell at less than its target price in certain geographic areas? (3)

To what extent do other suppliers follow the leader's tank wagon prices? (4) How much uniformity of prices exists among all dealers selling at the retail level, and what factors influence some dealers to set prices either lower or higher than those posted in retail outlets operated by the leading supplier? (5) Are dealers as free to post above or below the price leader's norm in markets where the leader operates a retail station as they are in other markets? (6) To what extent do dealers compete through nonprice incentives, and how far does the use of incentives having a cash value increase nonuniformity in net retail prices? (7) What is the impact of price on volume at the retail level, and does it appear that dealers cutting prices can by and large increase gross profit and/or net profit?

It will be observed that most of these questions are designed to shed some light on the issue of what type of price leadership was exercised in the Ohio market by the leading supplier [The Standard Oil Company (Ohio)], and how far this company actually led its competition in determining tank wagon and retail prices. Economic analysts have long distinguished between price leadership of the *dominant* and *barometric* types, with objections generally focused on the former, essentially because a dominant leader can establish a level of prices that is both inflexible and artificially high. In contrast, the barometric leader leads only by virtue of the fact that it performs a responsible and effective job of interpreting market forces.

The principal supplier in the Ohio market (commonly referred to as Sohio) has been classed as a price leader of the barometric type, and evidence for this conclusion has been built up through the answers to each of the research questions asked. Thus, in respect to question (1) on the leader's pricing policy and practice, it was found that Sohio's stated goal was to price at a level which gave due weight to all factors that might influence price, including not only those forces that might drive prices up but also those that held them down. Significantly, the company denied that it could hold an umbrella over prices, or get its target price in all parts of its state-wide market, or tie its pricing structure — especially in the short run — to its costs.

Company practice, which has been exhaustively analyzed, was found to be consistent with these essentially barometric statements. For example, tank wagon prices charged by Sohio to its more than 3,900 dealers and retail prices charged by its more than 350 company-operated outlets fluctuated down as well as up with changes in the business cycle, and while prices were raised mainly as a consequence of rising costs, such action was not taken in response to every cost advance or at the same time as the cost increase occurred. Sometimes, also, prices could not be raised and held at a level which would permit the company to pass on even a substantial cost increase — for example, in the cost of crude. These facts being true, it is argued that this price leader clearly had no power to dominate prices or set them where it chose.

Analysis of question (2) on the prevalence of local price exceptions provides further evidence for regarding Sohio as a barometric rather than a dominant type of leader. Owing to local competitive conditions, the company had to quote a lower-than-target price in 49 out of 88 counties between 1950 and 1957, sometimes, as in Akron, for a considerable period of years.

Analysis of question (3) on followership at the tank wagon level indicates that while on the whole major competitors followed the leader on tank wagon price, they occasionally showed their independence either by quoting a different tank wagon price or by offering a discount or allowance that resulted in a lower effective net price. In the area of jobber prices (which were at one time led by a subsidiary of Sohio), the company was challenged even more decisively and apparently lost its leadership entirely. And besides these few but significant occasions when the usual leader was ignored, there were some occasions when it followed other suppliers. There were also occasions when the tank wagon price had to be adjusted downward in order to protect dealers whose margins were squeezed by acute retail price competition. In short, the picture is again one of a company that led prices only to the extent that it did an acceptable job of interpreting market forces, and not by virtue of intent or power to discipline competitors and bring them into line.

Analyses of questions (4), (5), and (6), on followership at the retail level, contribute still another block of evidence in support of the conclusion that the price leader in Ohio was of the barometric rather than the dominant type. No more than half of the 99 areas intensively studied (in the Akron and Toledo Divisions of Sohio) were classified as having essentially uniform dealer prices (i.e., as having at least 90 per cent of the dealers follow the price leader's retail norm in at least two thirds of the periods surveyed). Even in areas where the price leader had a company-operated station, other dealers showed varying amounts of independence with respect to retail price quotations. The amount of independence is even greater if the group of deviating dealers is broadened to comprise not only those pricing either above or below the norm but also those offering incentives, such as discounts, premiums, and stamps. Since all these have a cents-per-gallon value, they could logically be regarded as the same as downward deviations. How much independence the dealers in any area might show appeared to depend on the economic characteristics of the market and long-established patterns of local price behavior rather than on the presence or absence of an outlet operated by the state's price leader. If, in a majority of markets studied, most retail outlets characteristically priced the same as the Sohio-operated stations, this fact appeared to be the result of competitive forces and of equal or nearly equal product costs rather than of leadership of retail prices by the outlets of the principal supplier.

In addition to permitting an analysis of price leadership in Ohio, the research questions elicited many additional facts about competition in the retail and tank wagon markets of the state, including some data not previously published and some findings of an unexpected nature. For example, in connection with the question on followership at the tank wagon level, a record has been made available of every price quoted (both tank wagon and net) by the five chief suppliers in Ohio in the cities of Akron and Toledo over a period of 68 months. The figures were furnished through the cooperation of the companies concerned and are believed to be the most detailed record publicly available of hitherto semiconfidential price information. The data provide not only a picture of the price decisions reached by large competing firms but also, still more useful, a picture of the way in which these decisions were actually made and of the considerations taken into account by company officials who performed the pricing function.

In connection with the question on the extent and causes of retail price deviations from the norm, that is, from the price used by the price leader, much has been said to dispel the illusion that complete price uniformity is commonplace in any retail market and to show that different markets may vary widely in respect to retail uniformity and difference. For example, out of 99 areas in the Akron and Toledo Divisions of The Standard Oil Company (Ohio), only 5 showed complete price uniformity in all the periods studied. In the 69 areas within the Toledo Division, the percentage of all dealers posting the same as the norm for regular gasoline ranged between 64.5 per cent and 99.5 per cent, while the number of periods with fewer than 85 per cent conforming was only 6 out of 15. In the Akron Division the above range was 58.4 per cent to 91.8 per cent, and the number of periods with fewer than 85 per cent conforming was 18 out of 21.

As to reasons for price deviations among dealers, these were found to include such factors as resistance to change in previously established prices, lag in posting changes, hope of using price cuts to increase volume, the competitive pressure of price-cutting dealers in the same or even in a not-so-close area, and the tendency of members of dealer clusters to price somewhat alike, that is, either over or under the norm. Other probable causes of deviant pricing were found among the characteristics of the individual stations. For example, very small stations tended to be sometimes above and sometimes below the Sohio norm — in other words, to show a pattern of mixed prices. More important, stations carrying private brands, if located in a city, tended to price below the norm, often underpricing by substantial amounts. Except for urban private brand outlets, an unexpected finding was that many deviating dealers had no consistent policy on price.

In connection with the question on incentives, it was pointed out that offering discounts, stamps, etc., enabled dealers to vary their real or net price to consumers even when their posted price followed the price leader's retail norm. Thus the number of dealers offering incentives had to be added to the number posting deviant prices in order to arrive at a true picture of the scope and extent of retail pricing independence. In the detailed analysis of incentives, chief attention was directed to stamps, and the findings demonstrated more success with this device than some persons in the industry had anticipated. Half the stamp-using dealers in the study appeared to secure enough extra volume to more than offset the direct cost of stamps, and stamps proved effective in protecting dealer volume even in areas where competing dealers had put substantial price cuts in effect. Oddly enough, stamps were sometimes protective against price cuts even when the latter had a much higher cents-per-gallon value than the cost to the dealer of the stamps he gave away. This circumstance suggests that the two devices for pulling in volume had a different basis of appeal and probably attracted different classes of customers. Finally, it was found that the proportion of overpricing dealers in the stamp-using group was not any greater than it was in the dealer population as a whole, a fact which suggested that the cost of stamps was not, as sometimes charged, passed on to the consumer.

While these conclusions all appeared quite clear on the basis of the evidence available, they are nonetheless advanced as highly tentative, on the grounds that the evidence covered only a rather small number of cases and pertained to a period when stamps were decidedly on the way up as a popular merchandising device. Also, owing to the fact that this incentive achieved importance only toward the closing date of the study, it proved impossible to make an appraisal of the long-run influence of stamps.

Analysis of questions pertaining to special regional prices contributed a wealth of information on how a barometric price leader studies the forces in its market preparatory to setting a price that adequately reflects the factors tending to drive prices either up or down. This phase of the study also shows the experimental nature of the businessman's pricing decisions; it shows pricing for the trial-and-error function that it is. Finally, and perhaps most important, this phase highlights and supports the authors' major thesis to the effect that gasoline prices, not only at the retail but also at the tank wagon level, are very strongly affected by the price decisions of a few aggressive price-cutting dealers characteristically selling high volume and more often than not carrying a private brand of gasoline.

Analysis of questions pertaining to price-volume relationships provides the factual evidence required for ascribing so decisive a role to the pricing policies of a relatively few off-price dealers. Their ability to pull gallonage away from competing outlets, and thus sometimes to break not only the prevailing retail price but also the prevailing tank wagon figure is documented with a wealth of data covering a large number of cases. While much still remains to be done in this field, the present study — thanks to the cooperation of many large suppliers — is based on more detailed actual records than the industry has formerly provided to economists. Even though the authors are able to raise a serious doubt that price cutting pays off profitwise in many cases, there can be no argument that it can attract gallonage enough to force many would-be normal pricers into retaliatory action. If this response is widespread enough, other dealers and suppliers must either follow suit or be satisfied with a dwindling share of the market.

A section on predictions and suggestions brings to a head a theme that runs through several chapters, namely, of what will happen when the price leader or any large supplier of gasoline in any market is sluggish in responding to market forces which suggest that a downward price adjustment is needed. The principal result of such action, the authors of the present study believe, has been to transfer leadership from long-established major brands to the more aggressive private brand competitors. The authors predict that this trend, already well established, will grow stronger in any market where major brand suppliers try to achieve a wider-than-necessary margin between their laid-down costs for gasoline and their tank wagon price quotations. Other and socially more undesirable attributes of such a market may include overbuilding, since new entrants are attracted by the hope of selling at high prices, and violent price wars in which the too numerous competitors fight through price cuts for survival.

In contrast, when the leading supplier tries only to play the barometric role of interpreting market forces and when the prevailing price is economically justified, the market is apt to be more stable. New entrants, present suppliers, dealers, and consumers all stand to gain in varying ways from the reasonableness of price and the absence of extreme fluctuations.

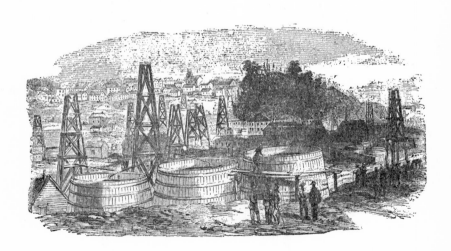

Competition
in
Technological Innovation

The Cracking Processes and Patents

by John Enos

MASSACHUSETTS INSTITUTE OF TECHNOLOGY

INTRODUCTION

Industries, like individuals, exhibit different characteristics. Among the most prominent characteristics which distinguish the petroleum refining industry is technological progress.[1] By improving its refining techniques, the industry has been able to process continuously greater quantities of raw materials and to produce products of higher quality at lower

[1] W. R. Maclaurin placed petroleum refining in that group of industries which has shown the most rapid rate of technological progress. "Technological Progress in Some American Industries," *American Economic Review* (May, 1954), p. 180.

costs. For example, in the 40 years from 1916 through 1955 the quantity of motor gasoline produced in the United States grew from 49 to 1361 million gallons per year; and while the average octane rating of gasoline increased from approximately 60 to over 90, the cost of producing a gallon of gasoline by the major process, cracking, fell from roughly 2.8 to 1.1 cents.[2] The increases in output occurred at a greater rate at the beginning of the period, but the increases in quality and the decreases in cost seem to have occurred steadily throughout. To the extent that it is possible to measure technological progress in petroleum refining, it appears that the rate has not changed significantly.[3]

Competition too can exhibit many characteristics — competition in price, in quality, in seeking new markets, in acquiring new sources of supply, or in developing new techniques. Like technological progress, competition is generally held to be beneficial, a socially desirable means toward the end of greater mutual well-being. It might, therefore, be interesting to relate the history of technological innovation in petroleum refining, in particular in petroleum cracking, and to observe the forces of competition at work.

Innovation in Cracking

Of the refining processes, cracking, in terms of investment and value added, is the most significant. All modern refineries producing a full line of petroleum products contain catalytic cracking plants, their capital investment representing probably 20 per cent of that of the whole refinery. Of all the motor gasoline produced in the United States, approximately half is produced by the cracking process.

Technically, cracking is a very complex process of which the exact chemical nature is still subject to some question. It consists of taking long-chain hydrocarbon molecules and breaking or "cracking" them by applying heat and pressure. In recent years, catalysts have also been used to promote the reaction. The major products of the reaction are gasoline and furnace or fuel oils. Also, small amounts of petroleum gases and coke are obtained.

There have been four waves of innovation in cracking to produce gasoline: the first reaching its crest in 1913, the second in 1921–

---

[2] These figures and much of the rest of the material are taken from the author's study, *Technological Progress in Petroleum Refining*, to be published in 1960 by The Technology Press. The years compared are 1913 and 1955.
[3] *Ibid.*, as well as "A Measure of the Rate of Technological Progress," *Journal of Industrial Economics* (June, 1958).

1922, the third in 1936, and the last in 1942–1944. Each new process or group of processes has been superior to its predecessors and has supplanted them in commercial operation.

The application of cracking to yield motor gasoline was first carried out in 1913. The variables which underlay the cracking process, however, were then well known. All of the basic principles — cracking under heat, the beneficial effects of pressure, and the promotion of the reaction by catalysts — had been discovered by 1900. Invention since then has been concerned primarily with the condition and the apparatus which would best facilitate the reaction. This work has required great imagination and ingenuity because the processes are extremely complex.

The first cracking process was introduced by the Standard Oil Company (Indiana) and named after its principal discoverer, Dr. W. M. Burton. Burton and his assistant, Dr. R. Humphreys, were employees of Indiana, the former a superintendent and the latter a chemist in its major refinery. They relied on their own initiative during the development, receiving little encouragement from the directors of Indiana's parent, the Standard Oil Company (New Jersey). Although the research was completed prior to the dismemberment in 1911 of the Standard Oil "Trust," permission to install the process and funds to construct the equipment were not obtained until afterward. The establishment of the Standard Oil Company (Indiana) as an independent concern, its lack of raw material supplies, the growing demand for gasoline, the respect for Burton by the local management, and the expected profitability of cracking explain the process' subsequent adoption.

The profitability of the Burton process was demonstrated within a few weeks of its initial operation, and Indiana moved rapidly to extend its application. Within a year it had installed a large number of cracking plants at each of its refineries and was processing not only its own raw materials, but similar raw materials purchased from others.

Indiana moved as fast to secure patent protection for the Burton process as it did to install the equipment. Burton's patent was applied for at the same time that the decision to invest in equipment was made, and, by coincidence, was granted in the same month that operation commenced. The patent revealed the art as it was to be practiced and, augmented by several additional patents on other aspects of the process, provided Indiana with a strong legal basis for its monopoly on cracking. A single process constituted the first wave of cracking innovations.

Firms inside and outside the oil industry responded to the Burton process in one or both of two ways. Some besieged Indiana with requests to license the Burton process. Indiana first succumbed to its former compatriot, the reconstituted Standard Oil Company (New Jersey), initially giving it foreign rights and subsequently domestic rights as well. The royalty rate was equal to 25 per cent of the profits from cracking. Later, oil companies other than Indiana's immediate competitors were permitted to operate the Burton process on similar terms. Two of the results from the first cracking process were therefore to establish the use of patents as a revelation of the art practiced by the innovator, and to permit licensing at not too onerous a rate by firms operating outside of the marketing area of the innovator.

The second way in which others responded to the Burton process was to attempt to develop cracking processes of their own. Almost everyone except those at Indiana recognized that the Burton process had technical limitations. It was not a continuous process. Burton and his colleagues were chemists not chemical engineers, so they were not alert to the disadvantages of intermittent operation. Indiana had a large capital investment in its own cracking process and therefore was not particularly eager to develop a new process which would make it obsolete. Moreover, the majority of the men who had carried out the research and development on the Burton process had, because of its success, been promoted within the organization and were now concerned with short-range operations. As a result, Indiana's research organization — the largest, the most successful, and apparently the most talented — was just the one that did not initiate subsequent developments.

In carrying out research on a better thermal cracking process, Indiana's competitors initiated the second wave of innovation. Within seven or eight years of the introduction of the Burton process, they had developed and were vociferously promoting a large number of continuous thermal cracking processes. Some of these were licensed as restrictively as the Burton; others, developed by firms which were not engaged in petroleum refining themselves and therefore were interested only in selling their process, were licensed to all. Observing the success of Indiana, all expected great profits. In such a situation, where the rewards were to be great and where there were many contestants, each firm gave great thought to its legal armor. Patents became mighty weapons in the anticipated legal struggle over the distribution of the profits. All the innovators had patents on their own processes, granted initially about the time their processes were installed. Not content with these, they sought and acquired earlier patents which revealed some of the relevant principles. Almost all of these earlier patents had been granted to individuals unconnected with the ultimate processes.

Of the four continuous thermal cracking processes which were to be the most widely adopted, only one, the Cross, grew from the research of the inventors whose patents were to be its legal foundation. Even in this case, the Cross brothers soon became inactive and their work was taken over by Gasoline Products Company, a firm organized to promote the Cross process. The other three processes — the Dubbs, the Holmes-Manley, and the Tube and Tank — were developed without reference to the original work of the patentee. Jesse A. Dubbs' patent application contemplated a process for removing water from crude oil, not for cracking heavy petroleum. Adams, whose patents were purchased by Texaco in order to provide an antecedent to the Holmes-Manley process, and Carleton Ellis, whose patents were purchased by Standard Oil Company (New Jersey) for the Tube and Tank process, were both independent inventors who carried out the research in their own laboratories several years before the innovating firms contemplated continuous thermal cracking.

For a while there was great confusion as one patent infringement suit after another was brought before the courts. Unlike the Burton case, where one firm held a pre-eminent patent position, the issue was in doubt. In order to prevent what seemed certain to become a debilitating struggle, a series of patent pools were formed, the first in 1923, about two years after the battle commenced. Initially it was the major oil companies — Indiana, Texaco, and Jersey — that exchanged patents; later some smaller oil companies and process design companies entered pools. The Supreme Court confirmed the legality of pooling in the Cracking Patents case.

Continuous thermal cracking reigned until 1936 when the first commercial catalytic cracking process, the Houdry, was introduced. Whereas the second wave of innovation was generated by many firms, the third, like the first, was the product of a single firm, the Houdry Process Corporation. In the course of his research and development, Eugene Houdry, the innovator, acquired patents on both the mechanism and the apparatus for catalytic cracking, but more as an adjunct to the general process of research. He, like Burton before him, believed that his process would be supremely efficient and therefore did not expect any competition.

As in the case of the Burton process, the Houdry process, although extremely original, dominated the art of cracking for only a few years. Its demise, too, was due to its noncontinuous nature. Again, it was someone other than the original innovator who demonstrated this. The Standard Oil Company (New Jersey) and several other major companies, when faced with the choice of adopting the Houdry process at considerable expense or of inventing one of their own, decided to do the latter. The situation of the late 1910's seemed to be repeating itself, and a reasonable expectation would have been the development of many competing continuous catalytic cracking processes. But the struggle of the early 1920's had left its impression on the major firms and their first act was to combine to organize a joint program of research and development. Houdry's patents were not thought to be a high barrier to the development of a successful process; more formidable were the technical problems. However, concentrating a great amount of talent and money on the development, Jersey and its associates — M. W. Kellogg Company, Universal Oil Products Company (the developer of the Dubbs process), Indiana, Shell, Texaco, I. G. Farben, and British Petroleum — came out with a new process, Fluid Catalytic Cracking, within three years. The first plant was installed in 1942.

The Houdry organization, together with Socony-Mobil, which owned a third of its stock and contributed part of its resources, replied in 1944 with the T.C.C. process, a continuous version of the Houdry. These two processes, together with Houdry's later version, the Houdriflow, constituted the fourth wave of cracking innovations. Since 1944 emphasis has been on improving these three continuous catalytic cracking processes, although if history is to be repeated, the time for a fifth wave is approaching.[4]

The Trend of Competition in Process Innovation

In an attempt to measure competition, economists customarily look at the structure and behavior of an industry. The industry in our case is petroleum process development. There are three types of firms which constitute this industry: those firms engaging in process development and petroleum refining (i.e., the major integrated oil companies), those firms engaging only in process development, and those firms having the potential to enter the industry.

[4] There have been some intimations of this, namely from Jersey, which is investigating the effects of radiation on cracking, and Standard Oil Company of California, which has announced a new process it calls Isocracking.

Let us first consider the structure of the industry. Prior to Burton's time, research was carried out primarily by individuals working alone on the fringes of the oil industry. Since then their number has diminished until few independent inventors remain.[5] The initiation of research and development following the introduction of the Burton process led to the formation of many process development firms. Entry into the industry by such specialized firms had ceased by the mid-1920's, however; their number has actually declined since then. The decline has been offset by the major oil companies which, as they reached appreciable size (to the point where they had refinery capacities of 150,000 to 200,000 barrels per day), began to do their own research and development.

Concentration, if measured as the share held by a certain number of firms, would appear not to have changed substantially in the last 40 years. By measuring concentration in terms of the number of companies, however, we would be committing two errors. First, we should not omit individuals from the calculation, for they too can develop new processes. Secondly, we should not consider each company as a single firm when it cooperates with other companies; the eight companies that developed Fluid Catalytic Cracking operated as one firm and should be counted as such.

If we allow for these two qualifications, our conclusion is that concentration in process development has increased substantially since 1920, and to the extent that concentration and competition are linked, competition has declined.

Another aspect of the structure of the process development industry is the number of suppliers among whom customers may choose. In the case of cracking processes, the number of suppliers has fluctuated widely: one in 1913 (or none if the customer was in competition with Indiana), more than ten in 1923, four or five in 1930, one in 1936, two in 1944, and three since 1950. If we compare the number of processes available to a refiner today with those available earlier, we find that refiners have a wider choice today than they did in 1913. Compared with the 1920's their choice today is narrower. Over the whole period from 1913 to the present, no trend is visible, and therefore no conclusion about competition is possible. Perhaps this is fortunate, for the number of suppliers is a less suitable measure of competition than the number of firms engaged in process development. The cause of this is the monopolistic instrument of the patent; competition in process

---

[5] Sinclair Oil Company, which tried to enlist the aid of independent inventors in the early 1950's, found the supply to be almost nonexistent.

development can be intense and yet a single supplier, the one with the indisputable patent, may emerge.

If we turn to the behavior of the process development industry in our attempt to determine how competition has changed, we can see two ways in which competition manifests itself — in patent and in price behavior.

In some industries patents have not been used; the inventor has practiced his art secretly, running the risk of discovery and imitation in preference to informing his competitors of his operations. In the petroleum industry the custom has been to patent discoveries quickly, revealing their nature in the process. Thus, patents have substantiated claims by the innovator to future returns from the application of his art. However, they also have fulfilled another function as weapons in a legal arsenal. In the 1920's patents unrelated to the historical development of their processes were acquired by innovators anxious to fortify their legal positions. Since the patent which is applied for earliest is most valuable, innovators sought patents from the past. When the battle lines were drawn, those innovators with the earliest patents (and the most lawyers), not those with the earliest or best operating processes, appeared to be the strongest.[6]

The formation of patent pools effectively removed patents as competitive instruments. Patents became tickets of admission to a club whose members behaved in a comradely manner. New patent pools have been formed as the cracking art has progressed, with the result that infringement suits have been avoided. Competition no longer appears in the use of patents.

The process development industry has maintained a stable pattern of pricing with all firms generally charging the same price and changes in price occurring quite infrequently. The royalty rate for the Burton cracking process was set at 25 per cent of the profits (equivalent on the average to about 17 cents per barrel of charge). Since then the rate has fallen in a series of steps, first to a range of 10 to 15 cents with the introduction of the continuous thermal cracking processes, and next, in 1934, to 10 cents. When Houdry's catalytic cracking technique was introduced in 1938, the process was licensed only on a paid-up (i.e., single payment) basis. On a running basis this was roughly equivalent to the 10 cents per

---

[6] Actually the issue seemed to hang on the contractual obligations of two individuals, Rogers and Adams, neither of whom had anything to do with any of the cracking processes. (G. S. Gibb and E. H. Knowlton, *The Resurgent Years, The History of the Standard Oil Company* [*New Jersey*], *1911–1927* [New York, Harper and Brothers, 1956, pp. 551–553.)

barrel that had been charged for continuous thermal cracking. The latter product, no longer so attractive, was reduced to 5 cents. Continuous catalytic cracking, when first licensed in 1943, was also priced at 5 cents per barrel. In 1952 the royalty rates for the T.C.C. and Houdriflow processes were reduced to 3 and the Fluid process to 4 cents per barrel. In absolute terms, therefore, the price of one of the chief products of the process development industry has declined by more than two thirds from its initial value 45 years ago.

In relative terms, however, the price of the industry's product has remained about constant, for the costs of other inputs to the cracking reaction have fallen in the same proportion. The royalty rate for the Burton process was 25 per cent of the profits from cracking. Today at a figure of 4 cents per barrel of charge the royalty rate for the continuous cracking processes represents about the same charge.[7]

On the evidence of temporal changes in royalty rates, we would conclude that competition in the industry is not very intense. Royalty rates have displayed an amazing stability, changing only four times in 45 years. There are qualifications to be made, however, for only during one period, from 1923 to 1938, were there ever more than three suppliers. The uniform nature of the price, therefore, is partly a consequence of the few firms offering competing processes.[8] Moreover, there is another dimension to price besides royalty rate, namely technical assistance. The licensor can assist in the design, installation, and operation of the process. Competition appears to crop up more frequently here than in royalty rates, although the intensity of this form of competition is extremely difficult to measure.

Looking at behavior, we find that our answer is by no means assured. As in the case of the industry's structure, our evidence points waveringly to a decline of competition in process innovation. If competition today really is less than it was 30 or 40 years ago, as indeed it appears to be, we might wonder why this should be. Three hypotheses can be advanced, each of which could explain this observation.

[7] This figure will vary considerably with the capacity of the plant, due to significant economies of scale in cracking. In 1955, according to the author's calculations, the royalty represented 10 per cent to 30 per cent of the profits.

[8] In 1923, when the many continuous thermal cracking processes were being promoted, price was used as a competitive instrument. Royalty rates varied from 10 to 15 cents per barrel depending upon the process and upon the size of the customer.

THE DECLINE OF COMPETITION IN PROCESS INNOVATION
AS AN HISTORICAL DEVELOPMENT

The first hypothesis which could explain a decline of competition in process innovation would be an historical one: i.e., that the industry suffered in the past from intense competition and had, therefore, changed its behavior, hoping that in consequence similar events would not recur. During the early part of the 1920's when the continuous thermal cracking processes were being introduced, there was chaos in the industry. For a while it looked as though all the profits from licensing the continuous thermal cracking processes would be given to a single firm. However, no one knew which firm it would be, for the choice appeared to be arbitrary. Each potential innovator was faced with the possibility that, if patents continued to be used as legal weapons, the firm which had carried out a major development might be deprived of any reward and the firm which had carried out a minor one, but happened to have a particularly strong patent position, would receive the major benefits. Considerable expense (about one third of the total cost in the case of the development of the continuous thermal cracking processes) was involved in obtaining the defending patents. It was realized that the rewards from research and development were great; it was also realized that if patents continued to form the basis for allocating returns, the distribution might be quite promiscuous. Given this risk, no firm would wish to allocate considerable resources to process development. Rather than encouraging, this would discourage scientific and commercial inquiry and therefore hinder progress in the industry.

THE DECLINE OF COMPETITION IN PROCESS INNOVATION
AS AN ECONOMIC PHENOMENON

The second possible explanation for the change in the intensity of competition in the process development industry is an economic one: i.e., that the major firms restrict competition in process innovation. In essence the introduction of new process is a disturbance and the large oil companies that carry out most of the process development do not want such disturbances. Order is a preferable state. The 20 or so major firms feel that they have reached a situation in the industry where the industry as a whole obtains as great a return as possible. Each admits that one firm may be gaining a little at the expense of another but believes that this situation is better than active competition. Each is content, therefore, to maintain his share of the market. This is what economists call tacit behavior; there is no collusion between firms, but each firm behaves independently in a manner such that the joint result is to maximize industry profits. The question to be asked is what behavior would we observe if the large firms acted in this way.

One way of answering this is to assume that the industry is composed of just one company. This monopoly would have many different plants corresponding to all the research laboratories scattered about the United States. How would the company behave in this situation? In order to maximize profits, it would try to be as efficient as possible and thus attempt to enlarge the gap between its costs and the revenues it received. In order to improve its efficiency it would develop new processes whenever it appeared that this would be more profitable than using the funds elsewhere. Since it might be wise to encourage research and development, such a company would use its research laboratories as effectively as possible, keeping each informed of the progress of the others. This dissemination of knowledge is precisely what a patent pool achieves. The monopoly would also try to prevent firms which might enter the industry from using its information by making its patents available only on an exchange basis. Presumably, the entering firm would not have carried out much research, and therefore would not have many patents to contribute. Thus, it would find it extremely difficult to gain access to the technology. A patent pool also maintains control by admitting to the pool only those firms that can contribute a substantial number of patents.

Simply because we find within the industry behavior that we would expect from a monopolist, we cannot conclude the firms in the industry are actually restraining competition. We merely conclude that the economic hypothesis is not inconsistent with the evidence.

The Decline of Competition in Process Innovation as a Technological Consequence

The hypothesis which the author is most disposed to accept is neither the historical nor the economic but the technological. The argument is that processing in the petroleum industry has become so complex that no firm by itself can develop a new process.

The increasing complexity of petroleum refining techniques is illustrated in the coverage of its patents. When the Burton process was first introduced, it required only three patents to reveal its nature and to support all the claims. By the time the Fluid Catalytic Cracking process had reached the same stage, 781 patents were required. Another measure of complexity is the total cost of the research, development, and improvement of a successful process. In cracking, this cost increased from $200,000 for the Burton to from $3,000,000 to $7,000,000 for the continuous thermal cracking processes; to $11,000,000 for the Houdry; and finally to over $30,000,000 for the Fluid. As a consequence of the increasing complexity, no innovator can avoid impinging upon the discovery of someone else. In order to innovate, a firm will require the assistance or at least the compliance of its competitors. Innovation must, therefore, be a joint activity and the industry must be organized so as to permit cooperation.

When this situation is reached, a patent no longer reveals a complete process; it reveals only a portion of it. However, it is impossible to practice only a portion. Therefore, when the technology is broader than the art revealed in a patent, the patent is no longer adequate. One solution would be to raise the standards by which novelty is judged. Another would be to admit that patents, which grant private ownership to minor portions of knowledge and encourage their restrictive use, are no longer appropriate for the petroleum industry. This the industry has done in effect by ceasing to use them competitively. In process innovation, patents no longer have any significant economic value; their major function is to provide social recognition of the contributions of institutionalized inventors.

LAYING OIL PIPES NEAR FRIENDSHIP N.Y.

The Recurring Spectre
of Pipeline Divorcement[1]

by George S. Wolbert, Jr.

SHELL OIL COMPANY

INTRODUCTION

Today, 145,000 miles of crude oil pipelines link 500,000 oil wells, located in 30 states, with nearly 300 active refineries manufacturing around 2,000 useful products from the raw material transported. Every refinery, not located specifically to receive crude by water or from an adjacent field, is served by one or more pipelines, bringing a variety of crudes from widespread sources.

Some 40,000 miles of products pipelines supplement short hauls by other transporters from refineries and water terminals and place unlimited quantities of high-quality petroleum products within easy and economical reach of 98 per cent of the nation's population.

There are 100 competitive companies engaged in the pipeline business; additional

EDITORIAL NOTE: Footnotes appear at the end of the article.

companies enter the field every year. Our pipeline transportation system is the envy of the world.

Criticism of pipelines today is sporadic and insubstantial. 'Twas not always so. In decades past, there have been proposals to re-organize the oil industry into functionally disintegrated components, and even further "atomization" into small size units was suggested.[2] Appreciation of today's pipeline structure is enhanced by a retrospective glance. As Mr. Justice Holmes once remarked, "upon this point a page of history is worth a volume of logic."

THE OIL INDUSTRY'S ROLE IN THE ENACTMENT OF THE INTERSTATE COMMERCE ACT AND THE HEPBURN AMENDMENT

Arthur Johnson has provided a fascinating documentary of the political-economic developments underlying enactment of the Interstate Commerce Act and its Hepburn Amendment.[3] Professor Johnson's book [4] attests the causal relationship between the resentment of the Pennsylvania oil producers against railroad-Standard Oil Trust discriminations and seminal Congressional proposals to regulate interstate commerce and to prohibit unjust discriminations by common carriers.[5] Among the early supporters of federal regulation of carriers was the Petroleum Producers Union. Its 1878 proposal,[6] introduced by Congressman Lewis Watson of Warren County, Pennsylvania,[7] was reported out of the House Commerce Committee as the Reagan Bill,[8] which, in turn, was modified by the Cullom Committee's recommendations,[9] evolving finally as the Interstate Commerce Act of 1887.[10] The Act required interstate rail and water carriers to post rates and to give public notice of rate changes. It forbade such carriers to deviate from published tariffs, specifically proscribed rebates and drawbacks, and banned long-haul and short-haul discriminations. Pooling of traffic and division of earnings likewise were denied to these carriers. Despite the fact that pipelines were not included within the pale of the Act, alleged pipeline abuses played a prominent role in its enactment.[11]

Two decades later, Kansas oil producers were instrumental in obtaining Bureau of Corporations' review of the disparity between crude oil and refined products prices.[12] This review led to the critical "Garfield Report," [13] brought before the Senate [14] at a crucial stage [15] in the debate on the 1906 Hepburn Bill.[16]

In both instances, the old Standard Oil Trust and its control of pipelines proved to be an effective symbolism utilized by those advocating expansion of interstate common carrier regulation to gain support for their measures.[17]

The Spectre of Pipeline Divorcement [18] first appeared during debate on the Hepburn Bill, due to the timing and language of the March 28, 1906, Lodge Amendment making pipelines common carriers,[19] and the May 7, 1906, Elkins Amendment involving a Commodities Clause restriction [20] against *all* common carriers.[21] However, the opposition of the House Conferees to inclusion of pipelines in the Commodities Clause caused the Senate to appraise carefully the results of this juxtaposition. At the same time, a deluge of protests from independent oil producers against inclusion of pipelines descended upon Congress.[22] This had a marked effect on several key Senators,[23] and when Senator Elkins, who had introduced the measure, argued for exclusion of pipelines,[24] the outcome clearly was presaged.[25]

After the Hepburn Amendment in 1906,[26] the Spectre paid only infrequent visits to the Halls of Congress until the Great Depression. However, during the 1930's and early 1940's, Capitol Hill was haunted by its presence. After World War II, the ghost left its congressional haunts, returning only once or twice in a somewhat desultory manner. The visages assumed during these visits included bills to provide for government ownership and operation of interstate oil pipelines;[27] to extend the Commodities Clause to include pipelines;[28] to authorize divorcement of pipelines from their shipper-owners under certain specified circumstances;[29] to prohibit stock ownership in pipeline companies by oil companies;[30] to prohibit interstate common carrier pipelines from transporting commodities owned or controlled, directly or indirectly, by the pipeline or by any person or company to whose control the pipeline was subject;[31] to make it unlawful for any person directly or indirectly to control, operate, or own any interest in any pipeline engaged in interstate transportation of petroleum products while engaged in production, refining or marketing the same;[32] and to define dividends paid by pipelines to their shipper-owners as rebates [33] prohibited by the Elkins Act.[34]

In addition to proposed legislation, there have been a number of Congressional Hearings and Investigations [35] which have produced reports [36] and documents pertaining to pipelines.[37]

The ghostly walks were not confined to Capitol Hill. Two Presidents delivered key messages to Congress urging action against pipelines. Theodore Roosevelt's annual message to Congress in 1905 and his letter transmitting the Garfield Report to the Senate have previously been discussed. On April 3, 1933, Franklin D. Roosevelt unqualifiedly recommended congressional enactment of emergency legislation divorcing interstate oil pipelines from other branches of the industry.[38] During 1938 Roosevelt appointed a "Committee of Six" to study transportation problems and to recommend legislation.[39] Among the Committee's recommendations was a bill to amend the Commodities Clause so that it would apply to any common carrier subject to Part I of the Interstate Commerce Act (thereby including pipelines).

Various administrative agencies have issued reports involving pipeline issues.[40] The most recent of these has been the series of annual reports by the Department of Justice on the operation of the Interstate Compact to Conserve Oil and Gas.[41]

The Judiciary likewise has seen the Spectre. In 1911, the United States Supreme Court ordered dissolution of the Standard Oil Trust along corporate lines,[42] which coincidentally resulted in separation of some pipelines from their former shipper-owners.[43] In 1940, the *API* or "Mother Hubbard" case was filed.[44] The complaint alleged concerted operation of pipelines to exclude nonproprietary shippers and to use the competitive transportation advantage thus afforded to control the crude oil purchasing market (conspiratorial monopsony) and at the same time to drive the nonintegrated marketer out of business at the other end of the line (group monopoly).[45] Simultaneously, three Elkins Act cases [46] based on a "dividends-are-rebates" theory were filed against companies selected to provide coverage of all possible ownership relationships between pipelines and shipper-owners.[47] These cases were compromised as a result of lengthy negotiations which had reached an impasse until Pearl Harbor forced both sides to accept a proposed draft with which neither was satisfied.[48] The result was the *Atlantic Refining Company* consent decree filed on December 23, 1941.[49]

The *API* case was held in abeyance during World War II, and abandoned by the government in 1951.[50]

Last, but by no means least, the twentieth-century glossators have had a field day on the subject of the alleged evils of major oil company ownership of pipelines and what should be done about them.[51]

SUMMARY AND ANALYSIS OF ATTACKS

Major Oil Company Ownership of Pipelines Allegedly Monopolistic per se

The most articulate spokesman against pipeline ownership by

major oil companies has thus expressed himself: "The chief weapon of the major companies for protecting their position in the market for crude oil is their ownership of pipe lines, the indispensable link . . . between the oil well and the refinery." [52] This type of thinking is based on *a priori* reasoning from the not insubstantial impediment to entry presented by the facts that pipelines require large fixed investment, are not duplicated readily, and that existing plants are economically efficient.[53] It is kept alive by a carried-over prejudice, conscious or unconscious, from the days when the practices of the petroleum industry had an unsavory odor.[54] Basically, this attitude constitutes an attack on vertical integration as an inherently evil method of doing business.

Vertical integration as a subject of antitrust examination has not been accorded extensive exploration.[55] But what law there is to date unquestionably holds that vertical integration is *not* monopolistic *per se*.[56] Nonetheless, once regarded as a positive good,[57] it appears now to be a neuter, a possible source of economies, but also of abuses.[58] It might be undertaken to offset the imperfections of the market place or it might be a means to control it.[59] If integration truly represents economic progress, the combined functions will be conducted at an over-all lesser cost than all of them managed separately.[60] Conversely, if integration is uneconomic, the total cost will be higher than that of the nonintegrated costs.[61] Normally, the presence of widespread integration indicates a market-place judgment of lesser cost, because competition forces acceptance of the most economic method. Dean Rostow disputed this conclusion in 1948 when he alleged: "Integration is not a means of achieving economies in production, nor does it result in such economies. It is the basic means of achieving and maintaining monopolistic control over price." [62] There is no reason to suppose that integration is *necessarily* more or less efficient in any given instance;[63] hence, it seems unwise to accept heated assertions in lieu of proof — we need to know the facts.[64] Possession of such facts does not come easily, it requires hard, grubbing work.[65] Fortunately, the "hard grubbing" on the broad issue of integration in the oil industry has already been done.[66] Professors McLean and Haigh in their monumental work on this subject concluded that the formulation and alteration of integration patterns in the oil industry *were manifestations of competition at work*. As the authors state, "it is apparent that if profits were easily won and competition generally soft in the oil industry, there would be no particular reason for a company to alter continually its integration arrangements." [67]

Although Dean Rostow was quoted for his articulation of the *per se* approach, he acknowledged its shortcomings in his 1952 article on *Entry into the Oil Refining Business*.[68] In this article he proceeded on the *assumption* "that the major companies could be found in certain market areas to have combined their market influence for the purpose or with the effect of influencing price and restricting the opportunities of competitors to enter the field." [69] These are typical Sherman Act concepts.[70] They are capable of being tried under the Act. In the absence of *proof* of these assumed facts, the basic argument comes down to the contention that separation of pipelines from major oil companies would [*they say*] promote competition, thus there should be a crime *implied* in order to fit or justify the punishment.[71] This certainly is a curious admixture of the *Mikado* with *Alice in Wonderland!*

Pipeline "Squeeze," "Subsidization," and Unfair Competitive Advantage

There is a three-pronged accusation here involved: (1) integrated oil companies are charged with raising the price of crude oil and depressing the price of gasoline in order to "squeeze" the nonintegrated refiners;[72] (2) allegedly high pipeline charges are said to bring "huge profits" which are used to "subsidize" the marketing phase;[73] (3) no matter what the level of pipeline rates, the nonproprietary shipper is placed at an unfair competitive disadvantage vis-à-vis the shipper-owner.[74]

There is an inherent inconsistency in the first complaint. Bearing in mind that pipeline ownership is charged with oppressing the independent producer and forcing him to sell in the field at prices dictated by the integrated buyer,[75] one wonders how even large integrated oil companies can manage simultaneously to raise the price of crude in order to squeeze nonintegrated refiners and depress the identical crude prices to oppress the independent producer.[76]

Adoption of the epithet "subsidies" has been a ruse to disguise the economies [77] and stability of vertical integration.[78] The "double profit" or "subsidy" argument has long been thoroughly discredited by reputable economists.[79] Dean Rostow, who can hardly be accused of bias in favor of the industry, forthrightly stated that the theory would not stand up under inquiry.[80] The reason is relatively simple. Integrated companies require a larger investment than do their nonintegrated rivals. Any advantage they might derive from being able to forego "profits" on prior stages, such as pipelines, in order to undersell competition at the final stage would require management to sell its shareholders on the proposition that there should be an abnormally low rate of return on the total investment.[81] If the marketing division were really unprofitable, it would be to the advantage of the integrated companies to withdraw from the field, and no amount of philosophizing could overcome the fact.[82] To the extent that pipeline transportation is more economical than alternative methods, the public will benefit, because in the long run competition forces the integrated companies to pass on to it a significant portion of economies.[83] The "bare bones" of this argument is the fact that critics object to integrated oil companies being in a position to pass some of the economies of integration on to the public in the form of lower prices.[84]

There remains the argument that no matter what the level of pipeline rates is, payment of any kind by a nonproprietary shipper to an integrated competitor places the former at a competitive disadvantage. This argument has been labeled a "fallacious assertion" by an informed and serious student of pipelines.[85] Dr. Stocking, also no friend of the oil industry, has discounted the argument as lacking in logic.[86] As long as rates are reasonable, and the independent makes no greater payment to the integrated line than he would be charged by a nonintegrated line, his ability to compete is unimpaired by integrated ownership.[87] Rates will be discussed in a subsequent section of this paper.

Alleged Exclusion of Nonintegrated Producers and Refiners

Industry's critics sometimes claim that pipelines do not exist to make a transportation profit, but solely to serve as a plant facility to carry the shipper-owner's oil. A corollary argument is that rate structures are designed to exclude nonproprietary shippers, thereby discouraging independent oil producers from bringing their crude to a refinery market and denying nonintegrated refiners access to crude oil sources.[88] The "evidence" adduced in support of these charges is the small percentage of "outside" or nonproprietary shipments carried by the lines.[89]

In analyzing these charges, one must first take cognizance of certain inherent limitations upon application of traditional common carrier concepts to pipelines — regardless of their ownership.[90] Pipelines necessarily are a specialized means of transportation. They are designed to transport fluids of a single commodity group — crude oil or products thereof [91] — in one direction [92] between given points of origin and destination.[93] Thus limited in capability, they necessarily are limited in their "holding out." It follows that potential shippers are limited to oil producers and refiners located in geographic proximity to the line.

The crude oil producer, like his counterpart in any other field of raw material production, desires to sell as close to his point of production, both geographically and timewise, as he can attract a buyer. For this reason, the producer *prefers* to sell in the field.[94] Why is this so? First, the price at the far end of the pipeline *at best* will exceed the field price *only* by the transportation charge.[95] Second, the number of potential customers will not increase, but the number of competitive sellers will increase the closer he approaches the processor.[96] In the meantime his capital is tied up.[97] There simply is no incentive for him to forego the convenience of selling in the field [98] and to undertake the cost and risk of going to the refinery market with his crude.[99]

Nonintegrated refiners as a group represent a limited business potential for common carrier crude pipelines. Professor Cookenboo has estimated the volume of this potential to be less than 4 per cent of total domestic refining capacity.[100] Notwithstanding the restricted number of potential shippers, it is important to examine how well this "public" is being served. Owen Clark, then ICC Chairman, testified before the Celler Committee in October, 1957, that the Commission had never received a complaint that pipelines were refusing to carry oil for anybody.[101]

There has been an admitted increase in nonproprietary pipeline shipments: [102] approximately 40 per cent of all crude oil movements reaching refiners are for companies other than the owners of the transporting pipelines.[103] Obviously, the entire increase did not come from nonintegrated refiners but they have shared in the expanded service. Every refinery in America today other than those designed specifically for supply by water or local production is served by one or more pipelines.[104] Nonintegrated refiners often have a greater flexibility of pipeline service than do their integrated competitors; i.e., they may have numerous long-line routing alternatives, whereas the companies that own these lines are generally wedded to them.[105] Not only does the nonintegrated refiner have a choice of long-haul pipeline routes available to him, but he obtains thereby a wide choice of crude oil sources.[106]

A typical example is the Clark Refinery at Chicago (Blue Island).[107] Ten competing carriers offer 19 routes from 13 crude producing areas (in 8 states) under tariffs in effect on October

15, 1959.[108] North and East of Chicago are the Aurora [109] and Naph-Sol refineries at Muskegon, Michigan. If local crude sources prove insufficient, these refineries can obtain crude from 14 sources and send it to Muskegon through 21 different pipeline routes of 9 competing carriers under currently posted tariffs.[110] Detroit has always been an active market — let's see what possibilities are afforded to the Aurora and Petroleum Specialties refineries there. Counting up, we find 17 crude oil sources connected to these refineries by 48 common carrier pipeline alternatives.[111] Over at Canton, Ohio, Ashland's refinery has a selection of 46 possible pipeline movements through which to draw upon 13 distant crude sources.[112] If this is exclusion, we need more of it!

Alleged Abuses of Pipelines

A sage observer of industrial integration issues has remarked that after losing the "double profit" or "subsidizing" argument and failing to show exclusion from the market, enemies of integration invariably fall back to allegations of "abuse." [113] Pipelines are no exception to this rule. Historically, the two favorite complaints have been high rates and unreasonable service requirements. Today, these complaints are seldom, if ever, voiced by oil industry people. Pipeline rates have shown a marked downward trend,[114] counter to the general inflationary movement of recent years,[115] including charges for other methods of transportation.[116]

Pipeline rate reductions have largely resulted from two forces. The first of these is an over-all rate investigation, initiated by the ICC on its own motion in 1934, producing a Commission ruling in 1940 that an 8 per cent return on valuation was fair and that 21 respondent carriers should reduce their rates so as not to exceed such return.[117] While this proceeding was pending, pipelines initiated a series of "voluntary" reductions, which had proceeded to the point in 1948 that the ICC discontinued the proceeding on the basis of a finding that pipeline rates had been reduced to a level less than an 8 per cent return.[118]

The second force has been competition from tankers and barges,[119] and a sharply increasing degree of competition between pipelines, accelerated by the development of large diameter lines.[120]

The magnitude of pipeline reductions has been substantial. In the 1948 *Reduced Pipe Line Rates and Gathering Charges* investigation Commissioner Aitchison noted an over-all average rate reduction of 43.2 per cent since December 31, 1933.[121] Rates have continued to decline since that time. Charges for West Texas to Toledo movement declined from 52 cents per barrel in 1953 to 43 cents per barrel in 1958.[122] Rates for carriage from Pauls Valley, Oklahoma, to Earhart Station (Detroit) have been reduced from 43 cents per barrel in 1943 to 37 cents today. Rates from the same origin to Canton, Ohio, parallel those to Detroit. The per barrel charge from Big Sandy, Texas, to Cleves, Ohio, has dropped from 63 cents in 1933 to a present tariff rate of 40 cents. Crude now moves from the Texas Panhandle to Houston for 21 cents per barrel whereas the tariff was 50 cents in 1931. Rates on traffic from Cushing, Oklahoma, to Wood River, Illinois, declined from 34 cents per barrel in 1931 to 21 cents in 1959. The charges on shipments from Healdton, Oklahoma, to Beaumont, Texas, have been reduced from 37.5 cents per barrel in 1930 to 18 cents per barrel at this writing.[123] These rate reductions have been widespread; this is shown by the reduction in trunk line revenues per thousand-barrel-mile [124] for all companies reporting to the ICC, from 61.39 cents in 1937 to 48.22 cents in 1958.[125]

Examination of tariff rates furnishes further evidence of competition between pipelines for nonproprietary traffic. Pipelines serving the same terminal points tend to post the same rate [126] despite the obviously differing costs arising from dissimilar construction costs and operational characteristics.[127] Another indication of such competition is the narrowing of the spread between the Mid-Continent-to-Chicago rate (which applies to largely *proprietary* traffic) and the rate from the same origin to Detroit and Canton (which are substantially nonproprietary movements) from 18 cents in 1943 to 12 cents at present.

Summing up, pipeline rates have declined steadily and substantially. For over 10 years no one has complained to the ICC that pipeline rates are too high.[128] The conclusion seems obvious: pipeline rates are fair [129] and reasonable.[130]

The other former favorite — onerous service requirements — arose mainly from a failure to understand the technical operation of pipelines which gave rise to many of the rules set out in pipeline tariffs.[131] As comprehension increased, complaints decreased. It appears that service requirements no longer are an item of controversy. There have been no complaints on minimum tenders or other operational requirements of pipelines since the early 1930's.[132]

There have been occasional hints that pipelines favor affiliated shippers by giving their movements preference, [133] in making connections, permitting smaller shipments, and by providing tankage.[134]

However, no evidence has been adduced to support these inferences. Interstate Commerce Commissioner Webb just this fall made the statement that the ICC had received no complaints of pipeline discrimination from independent oil producers or refiners, or from the general public. He added, significantly, that the Commission had ample power to act *if* such complaints were received.[135] We previously noted an ICC award of reparations in the *Minnelusa* case.[136] Hence there is not only absence of any proof of discrimination *in fact*, but adequate remedies are at hand. No wonder Commissioner Webb compared divorcement proposals to the use of a sledge hammer to drive a tack! [137]

Some producer complaints against pipelines have recently received considerable publicity. The basic cause of each is the same: lack of a purchaser to buy (at posted prices) crude oil produced by certain isolated wells. These complaints have been termed "pipeline proration" and "unconnected wells." [138]

"Pipeline proration" was the epithet placed on the charge that the productive capacity of some independent producers was being subjected to a limitation beyond that of the "allowable" established by the appropriate state conservation authority.[139] This group of producers (a small but vociferous minority) alleged unwillingness by pipeline companies to take their oil although they had no desire to *ship* it. What they wanted was a *buyer* — not a carrier.[140] Pipelines do not buy oil, and have not for many, many years.[141] Pipelines need volume, they are soliciting additional traffic.[142]

Hence, so-called "pipeline proration," which more aptly should be called "market proration" [143] or "purchaser proration," [144] is no creature of pipeline operation; it is against pipelines' self-interest because it decreases their revenue.[145]

The fountainhead of the publicity given the "unconnected well" problem by the O'Mahoney Committee [146] and by the Attorney General's Second Report [147] was the complaint by a group of Texas producers that pipelines refused to extend to a number of producing wells. These producers sought a general order from the Texas Railroad Commission directing all common carrier pipelines to connect any well whose producer requested it.[148] They also requested that all lines from West, West Central, and North Texas to the Gulf Coast be directed to increase throughput capacity in an amount sufficient to carry present production plus a "cushion" to provide space for oil to be produced in the event of a national emergency.[149] (This was at the time of the Suez crisis, when all pipelines to the Gulf were temporarily pumping at capacity.) A third request was for specific orders directing certain common carriers to extend connections in certain instances based upon evidence adduced before the Commission.[150]

The Texas Railroad Commission held extended hearings in the spring of 1957. These disclosed that the individual complaining witnesses were looking for a market for their oil and were not in the position of bona fide shippers tendering traffic.[151] The Commission found against the complainants' requests for individual connections.[152] It also found trunk line capacity to be adequate and therefore denied the request for enlargement.[153] It refused to enter a general order requiring connections of all wells in Texas, but instead established a procedure and criteria for adjudicating specific unconnected well situations.[154] In the 17 months from the Commission's decision in June, 1958, to date there has been but a single unconnected well case filed pursuant to this order, and it was withdrawn by the complainant.

Treatment of the unconnected well matter in the O'Mahoney record and report is purely derivative of the proceedings before the Texas Railroad Commission, because representatives of the sponsoring producers associations came to the O'Mahoney Committee hearings while the Texas proceedings were pending hearing on their merits, in order to obtain an extra-judicial, unilateral airing of their grievances.[155]

Likewise, the Attorney General's *Second Report* on the IOCC, which dwelt at length on this same problem, relied for source material on the record and pleadings before the Texas Commission in the case then pending.[156]

The unconnected well hearings focused attention on the *less-than-5 per cent of Texas producing wells* [157] which are located in an economic area beyond the line of diminishing returns for pipelines in today's economy. Let's take a look at the *dog* this tail is wagging — not just in Texas [158] but throughout the oil country, and throughout the history of the industry.

The history of extensions into new fields by pipelines can be appreciated only if one realizes the fundamental problem faced by any crude oil line; namely, the better job it does, the better job it has yet to do, because it is transporting an irreplaceable natural resource, and each barrel it pumps from present connections means one less barrel it has left to pump in the future. The only solution is to seek out aggressively new producing areas with reserves sufficient to pay out the investments required.

Each gathering line and each extension to a new producing area plays its part in the solution of this problem. Therefore, the pipeline's self-interest lies in making every extension and connection where the odds are in the realm of a business risk but the amounts involved (at $9,000 per gathering line mile or upwards of $70,000 a modern trunk line mile) preclude making extensions where payout cannot reasonably be anticipated.

The construction of these lines costs a tremendous amount of money,[159] of which 75 per cent or more is committed when the ditch is back-filled over the pipe.[160] The risks of losing this investment are many. The field may be a "flash in the pan" and the reserves may never be sufficient to pay out the line.[161] Recent examples are hard to come by, although every company has them, because managements are inclined to conceal them in the corporate closet.

Then there is the question of what size line to lay. The larger the line the lower the cost per barrel, *provided* the operation approaches design capacity.[162] But the total investment obviously is much greater. The question then is how quickly will field development take place? If the pipeline's "guesstimate" of reserves and development rate is good, the picture begins to brighten. If it gets too bright, you can pretty well count on a competitor or competitors arriving at the scene.[163] Add another risk — and a big one: geographic risk. Will other production be found more attractive to the refineries being served by the pipeline? If this risk matures, the economics are such that the more attractive crude will "back out" traffic from your line. This happens to every company in greater or lesser degree, but the most dramatic modern illustration is the history of the Ajax Pipe Line Company — twice struck by this same lightning, once in 1937 when the Illinois boom cut its volume back from 59,000 to 7,300 barrels daily; and the second time by a combination of newly discovered Canadian crude taking its Canadian consignees at the same time that the new Mid-Valley 22-inch line brought Texas-Louisiana and Mississippi crude to its customers on Lake Erie. No longer able to defy the lightning, Ajax hit the floor, this time to stay. It was sold on September 1, 1954, at bargain basement prices to the Cherokee Pipe Line Company for conversion to products service.

Finally, there is a technological risk. This operates in conjunction with the competitive element and is illustrated perfectly by the Service Pipe Line situation in the Rocky Mountain area culminating a few years back, when a modern big inch line had to be built to replace an antiquated multistation smaller line rendered noncompetitive by invasion of two competing modern "big inch" lines.[164]

It is the thesis of this writer that integrated common carrier pipelines have surmounted these risks in an outstanding manner. Those who have speculated on how these same risks would be handled by nonintegrated pipelines appear unanimous that the results reasonably to be anticipated are well short of the actual performance record established by integrated pipelines.[165]

MODERN PIPELINE FACTS

Entry into the Pipeline Field

From time to time critics of pipeline integration have "viewed with alarm" the so-called concentration of pipeline ownership in the hands of major oil companies.[166] The reported figures actually show a slight trend away from concentration.[167] Moreover, the use of "concentration" as an antitrust yardstick seems questionable.[168] The term is applied without distinction between an industry where 20 oil companies control 70.7 per cent of domestic crude line mileage and an industry where 3 manufacturers accounted for 96.8 per cent of the 1957 passenger car production. Indeed, "concentration" is a slippery term because of the difficulty of selecting a relevant market.[169] Concentration statistics are couched in terms of a nationwide pipeline "market." These have no economic or legal significance.[170] For example, Shamrock, with its 6-inch West Emerald products line to Albuquerque, has no interest in the ownership of products lines from Chicago to Detroit. On the crude side, a Gulf Coast refiner, such as Eastern States, couldn't care less about who owns Portland Pipe Line.

In the last analysis, monopoly or competition in the pipeline industry is based ultimately upon the issue of entry into the field.[171]

Most of the large oil companies of today commenced business under extremely modest circumstances, in a single phase of the business. Whether they started as producers, and integrated forward into refining, or as refiners and integrated backward in order to secure an assured supply of raw material, entry into pipelining usually has been one of the first steps. Integration has been embraced in order to attain the economies of scale and to improve competitive condition. These moves frequently set off chain reactions, and companies already in the fields or markets being penetrated altered their structures so as to be competitive with the new entrants. As a result, the pipeline field has remained in a continual state of flux maintained by a steady inflow of new entrants in various stages of their development. An examination of long line [172] owner-ship today reveals a remarkable variation. There are *Independent Oil Producers* with (1) wholly owned crude lines; [173] (2) crude lines owned on a joint venture basis with major oil companies; [174] and (3) crude lines owned by joint venture with parties other than majors.[175] There are so-called *Independent Refiners* with wholly owned pipe lines, both crude [176] and products; [177] and engaged in joint ventures with major oil companies in both crude [178] and prod-ucts lines.[179] We find pipeline ownership by *firms not primarily oil producers or refiners,* including: railroads,[180] natural gas trans-mission companies,[181] chemical concerns [182] and unaffiliated com-mon carrier pipelines, both crude [183] and products.[184] *Cooperatives* have entered the business, operating both crude [185] and products pipelines.[186]

Study of modern pipeline ownership impresses one with the remarkable ease of entry into the field. There is room for either small or large concerns to operate alone when the situation war-rants. There are joint venture possibilities which have made avail-able to the participants economies of scale otherwise beyond their individual reach. Firms with outside interests are penetrating the field. If ease of entry ever had any meaning in economic theory, the developing ownership pattern bears eloquent testimony to the absence of monopoly in the pipeline industry today.

Dynamic Development of Pipeline Network

One of the indicia of the healthy development of pipelines is the tremendous expansion that has taken place in the industry. The mileage has risen from 16,000 miles, capable of 81,000 barrels daily throughput in 1907 [187] to 145,000 miles handling over 10 million barrels a day in 1958.[188] Investment in carrier property of lines reporting to the ICC in 1958 was $2,850 million [189] as opposed to only $365 million of pipeline investment in 1921.[190]

More important than the rate of over-all expansion in size of the industry is the dynamic evolution of the pipeline industry into a vast complex of interconnecting lines linking a myriad of produc-ing fields to the relatively concentrated refinery centers.[191] A glance at the 1959 map published by the *Oil & Gas Journal* immediately suggests extensive interconnection between pipelines and innumer-able variations in the flow from originating field to receiving re-finery.[192] There are some examples in published literature. Bond [193] traced the flow of a gallon of oil from Gurley, Nebraska, to Toledo, Ohio. The entire movement was made under a joint tariff with a single through rate. The hypothetical gallon traveled 1,300 miles through four pipeline carriers for exactly 1 cent.[194] The Attorney General's 1958 report has two randomly selected examples, which follow the same pattern.[195] Our discussion of the nonintegrated refiner's access to crude sources provides multiple examples of interconnected movement possibilities.[196] The ultimate instance of the interconnected complex of modern pipelines is the movement from Poplar, Montana, to North Tonawanda (Buffalo), New York. Butte Pipe Line, as the originating carrier, posts a joint tariff on this carriage.[197] Two routes are available, each involving seven carriers.[198] What is the over-all charge for this 2,116-mile haul by seven pipeline companies? Eighty-one cents per barrel, or less than two cents per gallon!

A quantitative dimension may be added to this appraisal by examining the *number* of joint tariffs published. A survey of 48 crude oil pipelines publishing tariffs in effect on December 31, 1958, discloses that these companies post only 464 local tariffs, or 38 per cent of total, as against *752 joint tariffs*, representing 62 per cent of total.[199] The average participation for the 48 reporting carriers is 58 joint tariffs. Eight of these carriers are involved in single-origin, single-destination movement,[200] or straight-link of an international line, and hence are atypical.[201] If these eight are excluded from the sample, we have 40 companies participating in an average of 70 tariffs each.

So much for the possibilities, what are the *actualities?* The percentages of receipts and deliveries between crudeline carriers reporting to the ICC approximate *40 per cent of the total volumes* received and delivered by the systems.[202] This understates the extent of connected operations, because interstate lines receive substantial volume from sources not within ICC jurisdiction,[203] and a transfer from one company's portion of an "undivided interest" line to a wholly-owned line or to a similarly-held portion of another undivided interest line[204] would not be reflected in ICC receipt and delivery figures.[205]

A review of the evidence available on the subject of interconnection leads to the conclusion that pipelines today have developed into an efficient transport system, interconnected in such a manner as to provide the most economic movement for shippers in time of peace[206] and to render the necessary logistical support in time of National Emergency — all this without a cent of cost to the government, indeed paying tremendous taxes at national, state, and local levels.[207]

A second extremely important pipeline industry change has been the replacement of small diameter lines with large ones, usually jointly owned. Prior to the 1930's, the pipeline system consisted mostly of thickwall, low-tensile-strength pipe of 12 inches or less in diameter [208] and operating at low pressures.[209] High investment and high operating costs per barrel were characteristic. Increase in volume was achieved only at comparable increases in investment and operating costs.[210]

Shortly prior to World War II, pipeliners had become aware of the theoretical economies of large lines.[211] However, at that time the industry as a whole, let alone individual companies, did not have the traffic to support them [212] and it was only the stepped-up wartime demand that presented "big inch" theory with an opportunity to prove itself.[213] The same emergency brought a vital need for elimination of cross and backhauls and for the most frugal use of pipe.[214] The resultant vector of these forces was operation of all pipelines as a coordinated system by industry representatives under government directives. Existing lines were reversed, rearranged and interconnected wherever possible.[215] A number of supplemental projects were undertaken. Among these were the now famous "Big Inch" and "Little Big Inch" lines which established beyond any question that pipe manufacturers could readily make pipe of larger diameter, and pipeline contractors could construct such lines with reasonable speed.[216] The economies were crystal clear: capacity increases geometrically, almost by the cube of pipe diameter,[217] whereas investment rises at a much slower rate.[218] Thus, in order to double the capacity, investment need only be increased 40 per cent.[219] Moreover, proper operation of large lines results in lower *unit throughput costs*.[220] Thus, an economically balanced 20-inch or 24-inch line running at full load can move oil at barrel-mile figures of only about 45 per cent and 36 per cent, respectively, of barrel-mile figures in a well-designed 10-inch line of comparable length.[221]

Experience gained during the war with "big inch" lines marked a definite turning point in pipeline trends. More and more of the news lines were "big inch." [222] Over one third of present crude trunk line mileage is 12-inch, or larger.[223]

The handmaiden of "big-inch" construction has been joint ownership.[224] The throughput volumes necessary to attain the operational economies of the huge lines and the need to commit shippers to them has caused ownership participation to be broadened to the greatest extent possible. In addition, the traffic of those not interested in ownership participation has been most aggressively solicited.[225]

Those so-called "independents" who have undertaken participation in ownership obtain all the advantages of large-scale operation with a small-scale purse. At the same time, they retain their independence. To illustrate this, take the Rancho System, constructed in 1953 from Upton County, Texas, to the Houston Area. It appears to be a monolithic 24-inch trunk line but it actually is operated just as if the seven participating carriers each were operating a smaller line fitted into the larger line.[226] An analogy might be a number of wires in a cable. Each owner, on an "undivided interest" basis [227] identical to such an ownership of real estate, owns a fixed per cent of the total available capacity,[228] and each pays that fixed per cent of all construction costs and of all operating costs (except electric power which is apportioned on a barrel-mile basis).[229] Each owner posts his separate tariffs, makes his own arrangements with individual shippers, and collects his own charges.[230] Sometimes a prospective shipper finds it advantageous to compare the tariffs of the participants and thus obtain carriage at a lower rate from one of them despite the fact that the physical movement of all is the same.[231] If a shipper-owner of a participant desires to make shipments greater than the capacity of its subsidiary pipeline (or if other shippers' tenders to the participant pipeline causes proration of its "line") the participant may lease the capacity of another participant, just as it would lease a separate line. Or perhaps it might buy additional "line." Both of these events have occurred in Rancho.[232] A more temporary problem is handled by the shipper-owner, for example, Shell, tendering to another participant, say Crown-Rancho or Sinclair Pipe Line. The three independents participating in Rancho: i.e., Ashland, Crown Central, and Eastern States (Nantucket),[233] enjoy exactly the same transportation advantages as do the major participants. To me, this is but another example of the freedom of opportunity and flexibility of pattern existing in today's pipelines.

CONCLUSIONS

Specific Findings

1. In the early days of oil, as in many industries of that age, practices were indulged in which offend today's business morality.

Resentment against the use of these practices by the old Standard Oil Trust played an active role in early regulatory legislation and created the ghost which haunts the industry today.

2. Most, if not all, of the generalized attack on the major oil company segment of the industry has been based on abstract reasoning and carried-over prejudice from the pre-1911 Trust era.

3. Allegations of pipeline "squeezing" and "subsidization" will not stand up under inquiry. These objections basically appear to be against passing on to the public the economies of integration.

4. Nonintegrated refiners who do not desire to participate in long-length pipeline ownership have more-than-adequate common carrier pipeline service available which affords to them a wide choice of routes and crude sources.

5. Pipeline rates have declined steadily and substantially. The present level is fair and reasonable.

6. Service requirements no longer are an item of controversy.

7. Charges of favoritism lack evidentiary basis. There are adequate remedies at hand against any possibility of future wrongdoing.

8. Purchaser proration is not a creature of pipeline operation; carriers have no control over the matter and indeed suffer loss of revenue as a result of it.

9. Unconnected wells have received detailed examination by the Texas Railroad Commission which prescribed procedures and criteria for adjudicating specific unconnected well complaints. There has been no implementation of the order by any party.

10. The record of integrated pipeline extensions into new general areas of production has been excellent and has contributed substantially to the growth record of the oil industry. Students of the industry question seriously whether completely independent pipelines would be able to come even close to matching this record.

11. Entry into the pipeline business appears amazingly easy when the risks and capital requirements are considered. All manner of single and joint enterprises are represented in the field. Independent producer and refiner participation has greatly increased. Firms not primarily engaged either in oil production or refining have entered the field. To the extent that ease of entry is an indicium of the presence of competition and the absence of monopoly, pipelines pass muster with flying colors.

12. Pipelines are an efficient transport system interconnected in such a manner as to provide the most economic movement for

shippers in time of peace and to render the necessary logistical support in time of National Emergency.

13. Pipelines have changed their pattern of size and ownership in response to market place pressures. The economies of scale have been realized through a broadening of the base of ownership to the greatest possible extent. Nonproprietary traffic is being most aggressively solicited.

General Conclusions

1. Pipelines have enjoyed a fantastic development in many dimensions — length, capacity, efficiency and economy — under the present system; an interconnected network compatible with demands of peace or war has ensued. There is room for new firms and new techniques. Rates and service are unexcelled anywhere. The independent producer as a class is well served and the independent refiner has an adequate variety of transportation facilities available to him.

2. The present pipeline system has resulted in effective competition and technological advancement. The burden of proving that this performance could be bettered is upon those who seek divorcement.

Today's pipelines are like the regular player who has just hit a game-winning homerun. What better has the substitute to offer?

FOOTNOTES

[1] This was the subject assigned for delivery before the Centennial Seminar. Discussion from the floor appeared to indicate that a more appropriate title would have been "Laying the Ghost of Pipeline Divorcement."

[2] The most "recent" suggestion of this nature is found in Rostow, *A National Policy For the Oil Industry* (1948), p. 118.

[3] Johnson, *The Development of American Petroleum Pipelines* (1956), chaps. IV, VI, IX, and X.

[4] *Ibid.*, pp. 81–84.

[5] See also H.R. 2725, 44th Cong., 1st Sess. (1876), introduced by Rep. James Hopkins of Pittsburgh, on March 20, 1876. 4 Cong. Rec. 1812 (1876); H.R. 4004, 44th Cong., 1st Sess. (1876), same sponsor, introduced on July 31, 1876. Text appears at 4 Cong. Rec. 5029 (1876).

[6] H.R. 2546, 45th Cong., 2d Sess. (1878).

[7] Watson's proposal was made on Jan. 21, 1878: 7 Cong. Rec. 442 (1878).

[8] H.R. 3547, 45th Cong., 2d Sess. (1878); the Reagan Bill was named after Congressman John Reagan of Texas, Chairman of the Committee on Commerce, which reported out the bill. During floor debates on the bill, Reagan identified its purpose with the relief sought by the Pennsylvania oil producers against railroad discriminations in favor of the Standard Oil Trust. 7 Cong. Rec. 3280 (1878).

[9] S. 1093, 49th Cong., 1st Sess. (1886), introduced by Senator Cullom on behalf of the Committee on Interstate Commerce on Jan. 18, 1886, 17 Cong. Rec. 698 (1886). After recommitment, the bill was reported out as a substitute, S. 1532, 49th Cong., 1st Sess. (1886). Following lengthy debate, S. 1532 was passed by the Senate in amended form on May 12, 1886. 17 Cong. Rec. 4423 (1886). It was referred to the House Committee on Commerce, which reported it back in amended form, H.R. Rep. No. 2554, 49th Cong., 1st Sess. (1886). After a Senate "non-concur" vote, 17 Cong. Rec. 7818

(1886), the conferees worked out a compromise which was agreeable to both Senate, 18 Cong. Rec. 632 (1887), and House, 18 Cong. Rec. 879 (1887), and became known as the Interstate Commerce Act of 1887.

[10] 24 Stat. 379, 380 (1887), 49 U.S.C.A. §§ 1 *et seq.*

[11] On April 14, 1886, before the Senate sitting as a Committee on the Whole, Senator Cullom stated, 17 Cong. Rec. 3477 (1886):

The Senate committee, whose investigations have resulted in the presentation of this bill, present in their report eighteen specific causes of complaint against the railroad system, which may nearly all be epitomized as "discrimination" in one form or another. They cite among the many instances the case of Standard Oil Company, which has been enabled by railroad discrimination to practically control the oil supply of the continent, and who are reputed to have realized $10,000,000 in a single season from diminished freights alone.

A single instance, given on page 199 of the report, is sufficient to condemn the system. It appears that the company operates the Macksburg pipe line which carries oil to the Cleveland and Marietta railroad. This road was in the hands of a receiver [General Phineas Pease], who was removed by Judge Baxter upon the investigation of the rates charged for the transportation of oil. It was found that he was charging all independent shippers 35 cents per barrel, and the rate to the pipe line was but 10 cents. It appears that the Standard Oil Company owned the pipes through which the oil is conveyed from wells owned by individuals, with the exception of certain pipes owned and used by one George Rice, carrying oil from his wells, and to get rid of this competition the assistance of the receiver was sought and obtained.

The company offered to give the railroad three thousand dollars' worth of business each month, while Rice could give but three hundred dollars' worth. *If its demands were not complied with it threatened to extend its pipe line from Macksburg to Marietta, on the Ohio River.* What these demands were was stated as follows in a letter filed by the receiver as part of his defense:

"The Standard Oil Company *threatens to store and afterward pipe all oils* under its control unless you make the following arrangements, namely: you shall make a uniform rate of 35 cents per barrel for all persons except the Standard Oil Company. You shall charge them 10 cents per barrel for their oil, and also pay them 25 cents per barrel out of the 35 cents per barrel collected of other shippers." [Italics added.]

[12] The immediate vehicle employed was a House Resolution sponsored by Representative Campbell, of Kansas. H.Res. 499, 58th Cong., 3d Sess. (1905). The background of this resolution was the sharp decline of crude prices in Kansas ($1.31 to $.80 per barrel) in 1904, due to drastic overproduction. Kansas producers were unable to see why Kansas crude should drop in value while Lima crude remained at higher levels. They attributed the disparity to the Standard Oil Trust's control of transportation and alleged monopsony in crude oil purchasing. Johnson, *American Petroleum Pipelines*, p. 212.

[13] U. S. Bureau of Corporations, *Report of the Commissioner of Corporations on the Transportation of Petroleum* (1906), named after Commissioner James R. Garfield, who submitted it. The report's main theme was profiteering by the Standard Oil Trust through secret rebates granted by the railroads, but it also raised the issue of the Trust's pipeline power enabling the Trust to construct its refineries at market-oriented locations denied to its competitors by high transportation rates.

[14] For submission to Congress see 40 Cong. Rec. 6358 (1906). Johnson, *American Petroleum Pipelines*, p. 220, states that President Roosevelt clearly intended to use the *Garfield Report* to strengthen the case for the Hepburn Bill. He suggests that the timing of the submission was "more than coincidental." This conclusion is supported by a reading of Roosevelt's message to Congress relating to the Joint Resolution requesting the ICC to investigate railroad discrimination. 40 Cong. Rec. 3668 (1906).

[15] A synopsis of the *Garfield Report* was introduced before the Senate on May 4, 1906, when the Lodge Amendment to the Hepburn Bill came up for floor debate. 40 Cong. Rec. 6358 (1906). President Roosevelt's strong accompanying message stressed the Report's importance as related to the Hepburn measure. Significantly, the President waved the Trust once again as a red flag: "The report shows that the Standard Oil Company has benefited enormously up to the present moment by secret rates, many of these secret rates being clearly unlawful. This benefit amounts to at least three-quarters of a million a year." The full report was submitted to Congress on May 17, 1906. 40 Cong. Rec. 6998 (1906).

There is little doubt that the *Garfield Report* and President Roosevelt's endorsing message were instrumental in the adoption of the Lodge Amendment. In the Matter of Pipe Lines, 24 I.C.C. 1, 4 (1912); Sen. Doc. No. 428, H.R. Doc. No. 812, 59th Cong., 1st Sess. (1906); Johnson, *American Petroleum Pipelines*, p. 221.

[16] H.R. 12,987, 59th Cong., 1st Sess. (1906), introduced on Jan. 24, 1906. 40 Cong. Rec. 1520 (1906). This was a "clean bill" introduced by Congressman Hepburn as Chairman of the House Committee on Interstate and Foreign Commerce, reflecting combination of earlier bills and embracing Committee changes and consolidations. Att'y Gen., *Third Report Pursuant to Section 2 of the Joint Resolution of July 28, 1955* (1958), p. 58 [hereinafter referred to as "*Third Report*"]. The Bill embodied recommendations

contained in President Roosevelt's annual message to Congress of Dec. 5, 1905, 40 Cong. Rec. 91–105 (1905), and was introduced in response to that message. Sen. Rep. No. 1242, 59th Cong., 1st Sess., 2 (1906); Memorandum of Gov't. p. 6, *United States* v. *The Atlantic Refining Co., et al.*, Civil No. 14060 ("Arapahoe" enforcement proceeding filed in United States District Court for the District of Columbia on Oct. 11, 1957, opinion not reported).

The President's Dec., 1904, annual message suggested that the ICC be authorized to render decisions on the reasonableness of railroad rates, subject to judicial review. These proposals were contained in the Esch-Townsend bill of 1905 which failed to pass Congress. Johnson, *American Petroleum Pipelines*, p. 216.

[17] *Ibid.*, pp. 219–226; see also, footnotes 11 through 15.

[18] Divorcement, as here used, includes all restrictions on shipper-ownership of pipelines which deny some or all of the normal benefits which usually flow from such ownership, and invasion by government into the pipeline business in a proprietary capacity.

[19] See 40 Cong. Rec. 4375 (1906). The Hepburn Bill previously had sailed through the House on Feb. 8, 1906, by a 236 to 7 vote without any reference to pipelines, despite the pendency of a House Bill to make pipelines common carriers: H.R. 468, 59th Cong., 1st Sess. (1905), introduced by Representative William Randolph Hearst of New York on Dec. 5, 1905. 40 Cong. Rec. 55 (1905). Congressman Hearst had sponsored a similar bill in the preceding Congressional Session, H.R. 19,061, 58th Cong., 3d Sess. (1905), introduced on Feb. 20, 1905, 39 Cong. Rec. 2960 (1905), as had Representative Charles Scott of Kansas. H.R. 19,099, 58th Cong. 3d Sess. (1905), on Feb. 22, 1905, 39 Cong. Rec. 3127 (1905).

After the House had passed the unamended Hepburn Bill, but prior to the Lodge Amendment in the Senate, Congressman Rhinock, of Kentucky, introduced another House Bill to make pipelines common carriers. H.R. 15,438, 59th Cong., 1st Sess. (1906), introduced on Feb. 22, 1906. 40 Cong. Rec. 2881 (1906).

[20] The measure was designed to confine railroads to the business of transporting freight and passengers and to forbid them from producing or manufacturing coal and other commodities in competition with their shippers. 40 Cong. Rec. 6456 (1906). The House had a similar measure pending in the form of a bill, H.R. 15,329, 59th Cong., 1st Sess. (1906), introduced on Feb. 21, 1906, by Rep. Esch. 40 Cong. Rec. 2816 (1906). A somewhat similar amendment to the Hepburn Bill had been advanced by Sen. Clay on Feb. 27, 1906. 40 Cong. Rec. 3038 (1906).

The "railroad-coal" Commodities Clause movement had been under way for some time previous to 1906; for example, a special committee of the Senate had investigated the Reading Railroad-Coal Company tie-up and made its report in 1893. 24 Cong. Rec. 662–664 (1893). Thereafter, bills of three categories were introduced: (1) to regulate the interstate transportation of property owned or manufactured by unlawful combinations; see, for example, H.R. 2333, 55th Cong., 1st Sess. (1897); H.R. 1079, 56th Cong., 1st Sess. (1899); H.R. 3105, 57th Cong., 1st Sess. (1902); (2) prohibiting interstate shipment of articles controlled by a trust; see, for example, H.R. 127, 56th Cong., 1st Sess. (1899); H.R. 3131, 57th Cong., 1st Sess. (1902); and (3) to regulate the transportation of goods manufactured or sold under a contract or conspiracy in restraint of trade; see S. 1351, 56th Cong., 1st Sess. (1899).

[21] 40 Cong. Rec. 6455 (1906). Senator Stone of Missouri saw the Spectre on May 17, 1906, judging by his suggested Amendment to the Elkins Amendment in the form of a proviso that the Commodities Clause not apply to corporations engaged in the transportation of oil or other commodity by means of pipelines only. 40 Cong. Rec. 7016 (1906). He was talked into withdrawing his amendment on the basis that the language "who shall be considered and held to be common carriers" protected the small producers.

[22] Johnson, *American Petroleum Pipelines*, pp. 227–230; see 40 Cong. Rec. 9645 (1906).

[23] Att'y Gen., *Third Report* 59 (1958); Johnson, *American Petroleum Pipelines*, pp. 233–235.

[24] 40 Cong. Rec. 9250–9252 (1906); Elkins' description of the deleterious effect that application of the Commodities Clause would have on the independent oil producer was verified by Senator Long of Kansas. *Ibid.*, pp. 9252–9253.

[25] Interstate pipelines were included within the definition of common carriers but were excluded from the provisions of the Commodities Clause, which was made applicable only to railroad companies. 34 Stat. 584 (1906), 49 U.S.C.A. § 1 (8).

[26] 34 Stat. 584 (1906), 49 U.S.C.A. §§ 1 *et seq.*

[27]

Date	Bill No.	Congress	Sponsor
5/13/14	S. 5550	63d Cong., 2d Sess.	Owen, Okla.
5/14/14	S. 5559	63d Cong., 2d Sess.	Gore, Okla.
5/15/14	H.R. 16,581	63d Cong., 2d Sess.	Davenport, Okla.
5/16/14	S. 5584	63d Cong., 2d Sess.	Gore, Okla.

[28]

Date	Bill No.	Congress	Sponsor
12/9/10	S. 4480	61st Cong., 2d Sess.	Crawford, S.D.
1/29/31	H.R. 16,695	71st Cong., 3d Sess.	Hoch, Kan.
12/8/31	H.R. 172	72d Cong., 1st Sess.	Disney, Okla.
12/8/31	H.R. 420	72d Cong., 1st Sess.	Hoch, Kan.
4/15/33	H.R. 4681	73d Cong., 1st Sess.	Disney, Okla.
5/4/33	S. 1579	73d Cong., 1st Sess.	McAdoo, Calif.
5/5/33	H.R. 5530	73d Cong., 1st Sess.	Ford, Calif.
2/28/34	S. 2995	73d Cong., 1st Sess.	Borah, Idaho
3/10/34	H.R. 8572	73d Cong., 1st Sess.	Strong, Texas
5/17/34	H.R. 9676	73d Cong., 2d Sess.	Disney, Okla.
1/10/35	S. 573	74th Cong., 1st Sess.	Borah, Idaho
2/8/37	S. 1398	75th Cong., 1st Sess.	Borah, Idaho
4/30/37	H.R. 6794	75th Cong., 1st Sess.	Daly, Penna.
1/11/39	H.R. 2304	76th Cong., 1st Sess.	Daly, Penna.
3/8/39	H.R. 4862	76th Cong., 1st Sess.	Lea, Calif.
3/30/39	S. 2009(12)	76th Cong., 1st Sess.	(Wheeler, Mont. (Truman, Mo.

Senator Crawford's 1910 Bill, S. 4480, did not specifically mention pipelines. However, its language, making it unlawful for a *common carrier* to transport articles and commodities which it owned, would have encompassed pipelines. Moreover, a 1933 publication refers to an attempt by railroads in 1910 to bring pipelines within the Commodities Clause. *Oil Pipe Line Facts & Figures* (1933), p. 13.

Rep. Hoch's 1931 H.R. 16,695 is reported to have been responsive to depression conditions and the Association of Railway Executives' plea for "equalized competition" between railroads and pipelines. Beard, *Regulation of Pipe Lines as Common Carriers* (1941), p. 115.

[29] H.R. 5044, 73d Cong., 1st Sess. (1933), introduced by Representative Marland of Oklahoma on April 17, 1933, contained a provision authorizing the Secretary of the Interior to institute legal proceedings to divorce any pipeline company which failed to obey certain orders of the ICC, or which was found by the Secretary to be guilty of unfair or monopolistic practices; S. 1712, 73d Cong., 1st Sess. (1933), introduced by Senator Wagner of New York, eventually evolved into the N.I.R.A., 48 Stat. 200 (1933). Clause "b," Section 9, authorized "the President to institute proceedings to divorce from any holding company any pipe line company, which pipe line company by unfair practices or by exorbitant rates in the transportation of petroleum or its products, tends to create a monopoly." Francis, "Divorcement of Pipe Lines," p. 4 (Address Delivered Before Mineral Law Section, A.B.A., on July 16, 1935). Before any action was taken under this section, the law was declared unconstitutional. Wolbert, *American Pipe Lines* (1952), p. 4, n. 4.

[30]

Date	Bill No.	Congress	Sponsor
2/28/34	S. 2994	73d Cong., 2d Sess.	Borah, Idaho

In 1957, the O'Mahoney Committee entertained a proposal providing that under Section 7 of the Clayton Act ownership by an integrated oil company of a controlling interest in a pipeline shall be deemed *prima facie* a substantial lessening of competition or tendency to create a monopoly. Sen. Rep. No. 1147, 85th Cong., 1st Sess. 31 (1957) [hereinafter referred to as the *O'Mahoney Report*].

[31]

Date	Bill No.	Congress	Sponsor
1/11/39	H.R. 7136	76th Cong., 1st Sess.	Izac, Calif.
4/17/39	S. 2181	76th Cong., 1st Sess.	Borah, Idaho–Gillette, Iowa
1/6/41	S. 172	77th Cong., 1st Sess.	Gillette, Iowa
1/6/41	H.R. 1393	77th Cong., 1st Sess.	Harrington, Iowa
1/21/41	H.R. 2503	77th Cong., 1st Sess.	Izac, Calif.
1/26/43	H.R. 1516	78th Cong., 1st Sess.	Izac, Calif.
1/3/45	H.R. 55	79th Cong., 1st Sess.	Izac, Calif.
1/18/49	S. 571	81st Cong., 1st Sess.	Gillette, Iowa
3/8/54	S. 3075	83rd Cong., 2d Sess.	Gillette, Iowa
1/30/56	S. 1853	84th Cong., 1st Sess.	Langer, N. D. (Amendment to Harris Bill)

[32]

Date	Bill No.	Congress	Sponsor
7/8/46	H.R. 6972	79th Cong., 2d Sess.	Voorhis, Calif.

[33] H.R. 7623, 86th Cong., 1st Sess. (1959). The practical effect of this is to accomplish pipeline divorcement. Note, 102 U. Pa. L. Rev. 894, 912 (1954).

[34] 32 Stat. 847–848 (1903), as amended, 34 Stat. 587–589 (1906), 49 U.S.C.A. §§ 41–43.

[35] See *Hearings Before House Committee on Interstate and Foreign Commerce on a Bill to Regulate Transportation of Oil By Means of Pipe Lines*, 63d Cong., 2d Sess (1914).

Hearings Before House Committee on Interstate and Foreign Commerce on H.R. 16,695, to Amend the Commodities Clause to Apply to All Common Carriers, 71st Cong., 3d Sess. (1931).

Hearings Before House Committee on Interstate and Foreign Commerce on H.R. 5010, Crude Petroleum, 73d Cong., 1st Sess. (1933).

Hearings Before House Committee on Interstate and Foreign Commerce on H.R. 9676 and H.R. 8572, Oil and Oil Pipe Lines, 73d Cong., 2d Sess. (1934).

Hearings Before Subcommittee No. 3 of House Committee on the Judiciary on H.R. 2318, 76th Cong., 1st Sess. (1939) [marketing divorcement bill, but charge of "subsidizing" marketing operations from pipeline profits was raised by bill's proponents].

Hearings Before Temporary National Economic Committee, pursuant to Pub. Res. 113 (75th Cong.), 76th Cong., 2d & 3d Sess. Parts 14–17A (1939–1940) [hereinafter called *TNEC Hearings*].

Hearings Before Subcommittee of Senate Committee on Interstate Commerce on S. 3753, to Amend the Interstate Commerce Act as to Pipe Lines, 76th Cong., 3d Sess. (1940).

Hearings Before Subcommittee of House Committee on Interstate and Foreign Commerce on H.R. 290 and H.R. 7372, 76th Cong., 3d Sess. Part 4 (1940).

Hearings Before Special Committee Investigating Petroleum Resources pursuant to S. 36, 79th Cong., 2d Sess. (1946).

Hearings Before Special Committee to Study Problems of American Small Business pursuant to S. 20, 80th Cong., 1st Sess. (1947).

Joint Hearings Before Subcommittees of Committee on the Judiciary and Committee on Interior and Insular Affairs pursuant to S. Res. 57, Emergency Oil Lift Program and Related Oil Problems, 85th Cong., 1st Sess. (1957) [hereinafter called *O'Mahoney Hearings*].

Hearings Before Antitrust Subcommittee of House Committee on the Judiciary, Consent Decree Program of the Department of Justice, Part I, Oil Pipelines, 85th Cong., 1st Sess. (1957) [hereinafter called *Celler Hearings*].

[36] H.R. Rep. No. 2192, 72d Cong., 2d Sess. (1933) [known as the "Splawn" Report] has frequently been quoted for conclusions (1) that pipe lines are plant facilities in an integrated industry and (2) that "Commodities Clause" is inapplicable to pipelines. This report is also quoted for enunciating two (as yet) unanswered questions: (1) who would buy the lines if divorced? and (2) who would build to newly discovered fields?; Sen. Rep. No. 25, 81st Cong., 1st Sess., 2, 21 (1949) [*Wherry Report*]; Sen. Rep. No. 1147, 85th Cong., 1st Sess. (1957) [*O'Mahoney Report*]; Subcommittee No. 5, House Committee on the Judiciary, 86th Cong., 1st Sess., *Consent Decree Program of the Department of Justice* (Comm. Print 1959) [*Celler Report*].

[37] See Sen. Doc. No. 61, 70th Cong., 1st Sess. (1927) [Petroleum Industry — Prices, Profits, and Competition]; Sen. Dcc. No. 35, 77th Cong., 1st Sess. (1939) [Final Report TNEC]; and TNEC Monographs 17, 21, 39, and 39A could be termed private monographs instead of Congressional Documents, but they had a quasi-documentary status.

[38] Francis, "Divorcement of Pipelines," pp. 3–4; Black, *Oil Pipe Line Divorcement By Litigation and Legislation*, 25 Corn. L. Q. 510 (1940).

[39] The membership consisted of railroad officers and railroad union leaders.

[40] U. S. Bureau of Corporations, *Report on the Petroleum Industry* (1907); Interstate Commerce Commission, *Railroad Discriminations and Monopolies in Coal and Oil* (1907); Interstate Commerce Commission, *Conditions Affecting the Production, Transportation, and Marketing of Crude Petroleum* (1915); Federal Trade Commission, *Report on Pipe-Line Transportation of Petroleum* (1916); Federal Trade Commission, *The Price of Gasoline in 1915* (1917); *Report of the National Recovery Review Board* (1934) [Clarence Darrow recommended segregation, under Art. V, Rule 6, to prevent "pipeline profits" from being "used to finance competition against small independent marketers"]. For text of Rule 6, see Prewitt, *The Operation and Regulation of Crude Oil and Gasoline Pipe Lines*, 56 Q. J. Econ. 177, 200–201 (1942).

[41] Att'y Gen., *First Report Pursuant to Section 2 of the Joint Resolution of July 28, 1955* (1956) [hereinafter called "First Report," "Second Report," etc.]; Att'y Gen., *Second Report* (1957); Att'y Gen., *Third Report* (1958); Att'y Gen., *Fourth Report* (1959).

[42] *Standard Oil Co. of New Jersey v. United States*, 221 U. S. 1 (1911). Nothing in the opinion of the Supreme Court or that of the District Court, 173 Fed. 177 (E.D. Mo. 1909), indicated disapproval of vertical integration of pipelines. Hale & Hale, *Market Power; Size and Shape Under the Sherman Act* (1958), p. 205; Hale, *Vertical Integration: Impact of the Antitrust Laws Upon Combinations of Successive Stages of Production and Distribution*, 49 Col. L. Rev. 921, 924 (1949); cf. Att'y Gen., *Third Report* 66 (1958).

[43] The resultant vertical disintegration was more by accident than by design. Hale & Hale, *Market Power*, p. 206; Kales, *Contracts and Combinations in Restraint of Trade* § 127 (1918); Bork, *Vertical Integration and the Sherman Act: The Legal History of an Economic Misconception*, 22 U. Chi. L. Rev. 157, 160 n. 22 (1954); Hale, *Vertical Integration*, p. 924.

[44] Complaint, *United States v. American Petroleum Institute, et al.* Civil No. 8524, D.D.C., Sept. 30, 1940.

[45] *Ibid.*, pp. 37–41. The original draft prayed for pipeline divorcement, but upon the recommendation of the President's Defense Council this prayer was eliminated. *Celler Report* 142 (1959); *Celler Hearings*, Part I, 1263, 1279–1281, 1283, 1285 (1957); 86 Cong. Rec. 13,071–13,073 (1940).

128   OIL'S FIRST CENTURY

[46] *United States* v. *Phillips Petroleum Co. and Phillips Pipe Line Co.*, Civil No. 182, D.Del., Sept. 30, 1940; *United States* v. *Great Lakes Pipe Line Co.*, Civil No. 183, D.Del., Sept. 30, 1940; and *United States* v. *Standard Oil Co.* (*Ind.*), Civil No. 201, N.D.Ind., Sept. 30, 1940.

[47] Note, 102 U. Pa. L. Rev. 894, 905 n. 81 (1954); thus the suits were against a company operating a pipe line as a department (Phillips), a pipeline owned by several shipper-owners (Great Lakes), and a shipper-owner receiving dividends from its wholly owned subsidiary pipeline company (Standard of Indiana).

[48] For the full history of the negotiations as related by the able Secretary of the Industry Negotiating Committee, Charles I. Thompson, before the Celler Committee, see *Celler Hearings*, Part I, 1247–1664 (1957).

[49] *United States* v. *Atlantic Refining Co., et al.*, Civil No. 14060, D.D.C., Dec. 23, 1941.

[50] Note, 102 U. Pa. L. Rev. 894, 904 (1954); *Celler Report* 147 (1959).

[51] Black, *Oil Pipe Line Divorcement by Litigation and Legislation*, 25 Corn. L. Q. 510 (1940) [divorcement]; Cook, "Control of the Petroleum Industry by Major Oil Companies" (TNEC Monograph No. 39, 1941), p. 52 [government regulation of oil industry on a vertical public utility basis]; Comment, *Public Control of Petroleum Pipe Lines*, 51 Yale L. J. 1338, 1357, 1358 (1942) [government ownership and operation of pipelines suggested-divorcement recommended]; Whitesel, *Recent Federal Regulation of the Petroleum Pipe Line as a Common Carrier*, 32 Corn. L. Q. 337, 376–377 (1947) [government operation of "Big Inch" and "Little Big Inch" lines]; Rostow, *A National Policy For the Oil Industry* (1948) [vertical disintegration plus horizontal atomization]; Rostow & Sachs, *Entry Into The Oil Refining Business: Vertical Integration Re-Examined*, 61 Yale L. J. 856 (1952) [defends prior stand].

[52] Rostow, *A National Policy for the Oil Industry*, p. 57; Cook, "Control of the Petroleum Industry," p. 20, similarly stated: "Owing to their adaptability and advantages, pipe lines are the strongest means the majors have in competing against independents. The system as it exists today [1941] is a virtual monopoly of the majors." For authority, Cook cited U. S. Bureau of Corporations, *Report on the Petroleum Industry*, Part I, "Position of the Standard Oil Co. in the Industry" (1907), pp. 1–38. This was an investigation made in 1904 by the Bureau which found the main control of the petroleum industry to be through pipelines.

[53] Emerson, *Salient Characteristics of Petroleum Pipe Line Transportation*, 26 Land Econ. 27, 37 (1950); Cook, "Control of the Petroleum Industry," p. 20.

[54] Aitchison, *Some Observations Concerning Pipe Lines*, 16 ICC Prac. J. 232, 234 (1948); *Celler Hearings* Part I, 453 (1957). The similarity of language and argument is striking. Compare Rostow's charge with the remarks of Senator Lodge that through its ownership of pipelines the Standard Oil Company held "the entire industry of the country by the throat." 40 Cong. Rec. 7000 (1906).

[55] Rahl, *Conspiracy and the Anti-trust Laws*, 44 Ill. L. Rev. 743, 754 (1950). For a scholarly discussion of decisional law in this area, see Bork, *Vertical Integration*.

[56] *United States* v. *Columbia Steel Co.*, 334 U.S. 495, 521–3 (1948); *United States* v. *Paramount Pictures, Inc.*, 334 U.S. 131, 173–4 (1948); *United States* v. *New York Great Atlantic & Pacific Tea Co.*, 67 F. Supp. 626, 676 (E.D. Ill. 1946); Dirlam & Kahn, *Fair Competition: The Law and Economics of Antitrust Policy* (1954), p. 84; Wolbert, *American Pipe Lines*, p. 58; Comment, *Vertical Forestalling Under the Antitrust Laws*, 19 U. Chi. L. Rev. 583, 587 (1952); Adelman, *Integration and the Outlook For the Future*, in N. Y. Bar Ass'n. Antitrust Law Symposium 135, 145 (1951); Note, 58 Yale L. J. 764, 769 (1949).

[57] Learned, *Integration in American Industry*, p. 3 (Paper presented before A.P.I. on Nov. 9, 1949). The reasoning is that the shipper-owner relationship between refiner and pipeline has occurred with such frequency that it cannot be considered a phenomenon, but rather is a basic and natural combination of functions to achieve economics of coordination.

[58] Adelman, *Effective Competition and the Antitrust Laws*, 61 Harv. L. Rev. 1289, 1321 (1949).

[59] Heflebower, *Economics of Size*, 24 U. Chi. Bus. J. 253, 259–260 (1951); cf. Spengler, *Vertical Integration and Antitrust Policy*, 58 J. Pol. Econ. 347 (1950).

[60] Adelman, *Business Size and Business Policy*, 24 U. Chi. Bus. J. 269, 277 (1951).

[61] Adelman, *Integration and Outlook For the Future*, p. 136.

[62] Rostow, *A National Policy for the Oil Industry*, p. 117; cf. Bain, *The Economics of the Pacific Coast Petroleum Industry*, vol. 3 (1947), p. 17. In Rostow & Sachs, *Entry into the Oil Refining Business*, p. 912, despite a generally more tolerant view of the industry, the authors reaffirm Rostow's basic premise.

[63] Adelman, *Integration and Antitrust Policy*, 63 Harv. L. Rev. 27, 36 (1949).

[64] Sunderland, *Changing Legal Concepts*, 24 U. Chi. Bus. J. 235, 249 (1951).

[65] Heflebower, *Economics of Size*, p. 268.

[66] McLean & Haigh, *The Growth of Integrated Oil Companies* (1954).

[67] *Ibid.*, p. 674.

[68] Rostow & Sachs, *Entry into the Oil Refining Business*, p. 856.

[69] *Ibid.*, p. 869.

[70] Dean Rostow has never advocated *legislative* divorcement because he realized that the independent producer and refiner would suffer under divorcement legislation. Rostow, *A National Policy for the Oil Industry*, pp. 123–124. Hence his proposals sounded in the Sherman Act dissolution proceedings filed on a "discrimination against bigness" basis.

[71] Cf. Johnston & Stevens, *Monopoly or Monopolization — A Reply to Professor Rostow*, 44 Ill. L. Rev. 269, 297 (1949).

[72] Cook, "Control of the Petroleum Industry," pp. 32–33; cf. Edwards, *Maintaining Competition* (1949), pp. 98, 171.

[73] *Complaint*, pp. 39, 57, *United States* v. *American Petroleum Institute*, Civil No. 8524, D.D.C., Sept. 30, 1940; *TNEC Hearings* 7107, 7262, 7271, 7309, 7315, 7318, 7377, 7581–2, 8845, 8864–5, 8871, 8879, 8898, 9151, 9181, 9210, 10039; Bain, *The Economics of the Pacific Coast Petroleum Industry*, vol. 3, pp. 5–8; Cook, "Control of the Petroleum Industry," pp. 22–23, 28; Prewitt, *Operation and Regulation of Crude Oil and Gasoline Pipe Lines*, pp. 199–201.

[74] Rostow, *A National Policy for the Oil Industry*, p. 63; Rostow & Sachs, *Entry into the Oil Refining Business*, p. 883; Comment, *Public Control of Petroleum Pipe Lines*, 51 Yale L. J. 1338, 1341 (1942); 9 U. Chi. L. Rev. 503, 504–505 (1942).

[75] Cook, "Control of the Petroleum Industry," pp. 18, 24, 25.

[76] Farish & Pew, *Review and Criticism on Behalf of Standard Oil Co. (New Jersey) and Sun Oil Co. of Monograph No. 39 with Rejoinder by Monograph Author 4* (TNEC Monograph No. 39A, 1941).

[77] Adelman, *Integration and Outlook For the Future*, p. 141.

[78] McLean & Haigh, *The Growth of Integrated Oil Companies*, p. 176; *TNEC Hearings* 9748–9749; Farish & Pew, *Review and Criticism*, p. 13. It is significant to note that Professors McLean and Haigh found, on the basis of extremely careful examination (see principally chapters 5 and 6) that integration in the oil industry has been the *result*, rather than the cause, of variations in profit movement. *Ibid.*, p. 177.

[79] Comment, *Vertical Forestalling Under the Antitrust Laws*, 19 U. Chi. L. Rev. 583, 612 (1952); cf. Hale, *Vertical Integration: Impact of the Antitrust Laws Upon Combinations of Successive Stages of Production and Distribution*, 49 Col. L. Rev. 921, 938–939 (1949); Hale, *Size and Shape: The Individual Enterprise As a Monopoly*, 1950 Law Forum 515, 533 (1950); Bork, *Vertical Integration*, p. 199.

[80] Rostow, *A National Policy For the Oil Industry*, p. 65.

[81] Hale, *Vertical Integration*, pp. 938–939; Hale, *Size and Shape*, p. 533; Comment, *Vertical Forestalling Under the Antitrust Laws*, 19 U. Chi. L. Rev. 583, 612 (1952). Any firm, integrated or not, may do the same thing. Bork, *Vertical Integration*, p. 199.

[82] Farish & Pew, *Review and Criticism*, p. 12.

[83] Emerson, *Salient Characteristics of Petroleum Pipe Line Transportation*, p. 39.

[84] Beaton, *Enterprise in Oil* (1957), p. 483; cf. *Petroleum Rail Shippers' Ass'n* v. *Alton & Southern R.R.*, 243 ICC 589, 629 (1941). Dean Rostow comments "Small and medium-sized business has more freedom in a sellers' market to charge what the market will bear. It is less concerned than big business with the public relations and antitrust implications of increases in price or in capacity." Rostow, *Problems of Size and Integration* in N. Y. Bar Ass'n Antitrust Law Symposium 117, 118 (1951). See also Farish & Pew *Review and Criticism*, p. 55.

[85] Cookenboo, *Crude Oil Pipe Lines and Competition in the Oil Industry* (1955), p. 104.

[86] Stocking, Book Review, 1 Vand. L. Rev. 490, 492 (1948) [Reviewing Rostow's *A National Policy For the Oil Industry*].

[87] Cookenboo, *Crude Oil Pipe Lines*, p. 104; Wolbert, *American Pipe Lines*, p. 58; Note, 102 U. Pa. L. Rev. 894, 912 (1954); Bork, *Vertical Integration*, p. 200.

[88] Rostow, *A National Policy For the Oil Industry*, p. 62 (producers); Comment, *Public Control of Petroleum Pipe Lines*, pp. 1338, 1340 (refiners); *Celler Report* 124–125 (1959); *O'Mahoney Report* 28 (1957) [producers]; *Wherry Report* 10, 20 (1949) [refiners].

[89] See Wolbert, *American Pipe Lines*, pp. 43–45, for a description of this data.

[90] The *Celler Report* (1959), p. 124, attempts to apply such concepts to pipelines: "The percentage of outside shipments still remains substantially lower than is normally associated with common carriage transportation."

[91] Emerson, *Salient Characteristics of Petroleum Pipe Line Transportation*, 26 Land Econ. 27 (1950); Webb, *ICC Regulation of the Oil Industry* (1959), p. 5; Kinsolving, *Underground Rivers of Oil* (A.P.I. Oil Industry Background Information Bull. No. 7, 1954), p. 6. Pipelines are not used interchangeably for crude and products because the problems of contamination are too serious. Emerson, *Salient Characteristics*, p. 57.

[92] Frequently, pipelines are tapered from beginning to end so that the diameter increases (crude lines) or decreases (products lines) progressively. This presents a practical impediment to reversal of flow, although change has taken place, notably in the case of Tuscarora, which altered both direction and type of commodity carried in 1930. McLean & Haigh, *The Growth of Integrated Oil Companies*, pp. 207–208; Spal, *Oil Pipe Lines*, 15 ICC Prac. J. 563, 565 (1948).

[93] Bain, *The Economics of the Pacific Coast Petroleum Industry*, vol. 1 (1944), p. 76; Bond, *Oil Pipelines — Their Operation and Regulation*, 25 ICC Prac. J. 730, 740 (1958); *Celler Hearings* 449, 1135 (1957); *O'Mahoney Report* 131 (1957).

94 Wolbert, *American Pipe Lines*, p. 265; Hamilton, *Competition in Oil* (1958), p. 5; *O'Mahoney Report* 129 (1957) [minority report citing letter of June 24, 1957, from the Independent Petroleum Association of America to the Committee Chairman].

95 Farish & Pew, *Review and Criticism*, p. 32; Bain, *The Economics of the Pacific Coast Petroleum Industry*, vol. 3, p. 46; cf. Att'y Gen., *Second Report* 75 (1957).

96 Cookenboo, *Crude Oil Pipe Lines*, p. 94.

97 Wolbert, *American Pipe Lines*, p. 47.

98 *Wherry Report* 20 (1949).

99 Cf. Att'y Gen., *Third Report* 59 (1958).

100 Cookenboo, *Crude Oil Pipe Lines*, pp. 114–119.

101 *Celler Hearings* 451 (1957).

102 Rostow & Sachs, *Entry into the Oil Refining Business*, p. 893; *Celler Report* 124 (1959); Wolbert, *American Pipe Lines*, p. 45.

103 *O'Mahoney Report* 131 (1957).

104 *Celler Report* 124 (1959); *Celler Hearings* 1136 (1957); "Map, Crude Oil Pipelines and Principal Refineries," *Oil & Gas Journal* (Sept. 21, 1959).

105 *O'Mahoney Report* 131 (1957). An example of this was furnished by one of the complainant witnesses before the TNEC. Mr. Louis J. Walsh, an independent refiner from Houston, testified that his company owned no pipelines nor any production but he was connected to the pipelines of three major companies. By this method, with which he had no trouble, he had crude available from practically all the fields in Texas and New Mexico, and some fields in Louisiana. *TNEC Hearings 7337*.

106 *Celler Report* 124 (1959); *Celler Hearings* 1136 (1957).

107 In Rostow & Sachs, *Entry into the Oil Refining Business*, pp. 891–892, the authors cited the case of another Chicago nonintegrated refiner — Globe Oil & Refinery Company — for the proposition that a well-managed "independent" refining company had been able to thrive on common carrier pipeline service. These remarks about Clark would have applied equally to Globe.

108 Common Carrier Crude Oil Pipe Line Transportation

Available to Clark Refinery at Chicago, Illinois

As of October 15, 1959

Sources of Crude Oil Production Available	Applicable Rates in Cents per Barrel		Tariffs Published by	ICC No.
	Trunk	Gathering		
Oklahoma	25	10	⌠Sinclair ⌡Cherokee	246 47, 49, 50
Kansas	24	10	⌠Arapahoe ⌡Sinclair	71 246
Kansas (Brown County)	31-½		Platte	176
North Texas	25	10	⌠Continental ⌡Texas	74 537
North Central Texas	26		Shell	556
West Central Texas	29	5	Shell	591(2),a 592
West Texas and New Mexico	33	5	Texas-New Mexico	315(2) a
Colorado and Nebraska	32	10	⌠Arapahoe ⟨Platte ⌡Toronto	74 211 75
Eastern Montana	56	7	Butte	61
Wyoming	35		Platte	211
Texas (Grayson County)	30	5	Texas	539

a Figures in parentheses indicate number of different routes.

109 Aurora has been purchased recently by the Ohio Oil Company, but its use at this writing, for illustrative purposes based on its history of successful operation involving reliance on common carrier pipeline service, appears valid.

Common Carrier Crude Oil Pipe Line Transportation

Available to Aurora and Naph-Sol Refineries at Muskegon, Michigan

As of October 15, 1959

Sources of Crude Oil Production Available	Applicable Rates in Cents per Barrel		Tariffs	
	Trunk [a]	Gathering	Published by [b]	ICC No.
Oklahoma	42	10	Service	333
			Sinclair	162, 242
Kansas	41	10	Arapahoe	73
Kansas	42	10	Service	333
North Texas	42	10	Texas-New Mexico	312
West Texas and New Mexico	52	5	Service	364
West Texas and New Mexico	50	5	Texas-New Mexico	312(2) [c]
Texas Panhandle	50		Phillips	64, 79
Colorado	49	10	Arapahoe	117
Nebraska	49	10	Arapahoe	117
			Platte	194, 213(2) [c]
Eastern Wyoming	52	5	Platte	213(2)
			Service	338
Western Wyoming	54	5	Ohio	A-580(2) [c]
			Platte	164, 194
			Service	308
Lance Creek, Wyoming	53		Platte	189
Eastern Montana	73	7	Butte	64
Illinois	29-½		Texaco-Cities Service	31

[a] Total combined rate including Muskegon Pipe Line's 17-cent local rate from Griffith, Indiana, to Muskegon, Michigan.
[b] Companies indicated publish tariffs to Griffith, Indiana. Movement from Griffith to Muskegon covered by local tariff published by Muskegon Pipe Line Company.
[c] Figures in parentheses indicate number of different routes.

Common Carrier Crude Oil Pipe Line Transportation

Available to Aurora and Petroleum Specialties Refineries at Detroit

As of October 15, 1959

Sources of Crude Oil Production Available	Applicable Rates in Cents per Barrel		Tariffs	
	Trunk	Gathering	Published by	ICC No.
Oklahoma	37	10	Service	260
			Sinclair	191
Oklahoma (Purcell)	40	10	Magnolia	A-501(4) [a]
Kansas	37	10	Arapahoe	98, 114, 134
			Service	332
North Texas	40	10	Magnolia	A-501(4) [a]
West Central Texas	47		Magnolia	A-501(4) [a]
Scurry, Texas	49	5	Magnolia	A-501(4) [a]
West Texas	47	5	Service	264
West Texas (Fullerton)	52	5	Magnolia	A-501(4) [a]
New Mexico	52	5	Magnolia	A-501(4) [a]
Colorado	44	10	Arapahoe	87(2),[a] 103
			Service	265
			Toronto	78(2),[a] 83
Nebraska	44	10	Arapahoe	87(2),[a] 103
			Platte	171(2),[a] 196
			Service	265
			Toronto	78(2),[a] 83

132   OIL'S FIRST CENTURY

Sources	Trunk	Gathering	Published by	ICC No.
Western Wyoming	49	5	Ohio	A-573, A-585
			Platte	151(2),[a] 158,
				168, 187, 212
			Service	262, 273, 315
Eastern Wyoming	47		Platte	151, 153, 191
Lance Creek, Wyoming	48		Platte	197
Eastern Montana	68	7	Butte	62, 68, 70
Illinois	20	10	Interstate	570, 580
			Ohio	A-469, A-470
			Pure	240
			Texaco-Cities	
			Service	6, 10
			Texas	511, 521, 550
Indiana	20		Ohio	A-469, A-470
Montana (Carbon Co.)	49	5	Ohio	A-585

[a] Figures in parentheses indicate number of different routes.

[112] Common Carrier Crude Oil Pipe Line Transportation

Available to Ashland Refinery at Canton, Ohio

As of October 15, 1959

Sources of Crude Oil Production Available	Applicable Rates in Cents per Barrel		Tariffs	
	Trunk	Gathering	Published by	ICC No.
Oklahoma	37	10	Service	260(2)[a]
			Sinclair	169(2),[a] 189
Kansas	37	10	Arapahoe	107, 93(2)[a]
North Central Texas	38		Shell	547
West Texas	47	5	Ashland	14(2),[a] 16
			Service	264(2)[a]
			Shell	516
			Sinclair	178(2),[a] 188(2)[a]
West Texas	50	5	Texas-New Mexico	260(7)[a]
New Mexico	50	5	Texas-New Mexico	260(4)[a]
Colorado and Nebraska	44	10	Arapahoe	85(2),[a] 101
			Service	265(2)[a]
			Toronto	76
Western Wyoming	49	5	Platte	202
			Service	262
East Texas	25-¼		Mid-Valley	74
Illinois	20	10	Ashland	9
			Interstate	569
			Ohio	A-440, A-562
			Pure	230
			Texaco-Cities	
			Service	12, 22
			Texas	481
Indiana	20		Ohio	A-562
Kentucky	22		Ohio	A-560

[a] Figures in parentheses indicate number of different routes.

[113] Hale, *Vertical Integration*, p. 948.
[114] *Reduced Pipe Line Rates and Gathering Charges*, 272 ICC 375, 380, 384 (1948).
[115] *Celler Hearings* 453, 1136 (1957); Aitchison, *Some Observations Concerning Pipe Lines*, 16 ICC Prac. J. 232, 233 (1948).
[116] *Reduced Pipe Line Rates and Gathering Charges*, 272 ICC 375, 384 (1948); *Celler Hearings* 1136 (1957); Bond, *Oil Pipelines*, p. 739; Rostow & Sachs, *Entry into the Oil Refining Business*, p. 858; cf. *Wherry Report* 20 (1947).
[117] *Reduced Pipe Line Rates and Gathering Charges*, 243 ICC 115, 142–144 (1940).
[118] *Ibid.*, 272 ICC 375 (1948). These "voluntary" reductions certainly were not impeded by the action of the ICC in granting reparations to a pipeline shipper in *Minnelusa Oil Corp. v. Continental Pipe Line Co.*, 258 ICC 41 (1948). It also is a matter of differing opinion among pipeliners whether or not the *Atlantic Refining Company* consent decree has played a part in this movement.

119 McLean & Haigh, *The Growth of Integrated Oil Companies*, p. 194; Note, 102 U. Pa. L. Rev. 894, 903 (1954); Farish & Pew, *Review and Criticism*, p. 34; Wolbert, *American Pipe Lines*, p. 16.

120 McLean & Haigh, *The Growth of Integrated Oil Companies*, p. 194; Note, 102 U. Pa. L. Rev. 894, 903 (1954); *Celler Hearings* 1135–1136 (1957); cf. Bond, *Oil Pipelines*, p. 739.

121 *Reduced Pipe Line Rates and Gathering Charges*, 272 ICC 375, 381 (1948).

122 Bond, *Oil Pipelines*, p. 741.

123 These specific illustrations were furnished at the writer's request by R. J. Andress, Executive Vice President, Service Pipe Line Company under letter dated October 27, 1959; source was tariffs filed with ICC.

124 The 1,000-barrel-mile standard was chosen to eliminate the effect of the trend toward increased length of haul. Spal, *Oil Pipe Lines*, 15 ICC Prac. J. 563, 567 (1948). This has gone from 253.3 miles in 1940 to 300.2 miles in 1948.

125 Trunk Transportation Revenue per 1,000-barrel-mile.

1937	61.39	1948	45.70
1938	61.39	1949	47.43
1939	56.55	1950	48.15
1940	56.09	1951	48.30
1941	53.90	1952	50.03
1942	47.96	1953	49.05
1943	46.95	1954	48.55
1944	46.99	1955	49.05
1945	46.90	1956	48.25
1946	44.84	1957	47.47
1947	44.66	1958	48.22

SOURCE: Computed from annual Oil Pipe Line Statistics prepared by Bureau of Transport Economics and Statistics, Interstate Commerce Commission. Cf. Cookenboo, *Crude Oil Pipe Lines*, p. 101. Discrepancy between these figures and Cookenboo's 1952 and 1953 figures is due to the fact he used total trunkline revenue (including storage, demurrage, and rent) whereas above figures are strictly transportation revenue.

126 See tariff rates in footnotes 108, 110, 111, and 112.

127 This bears out Commissioner Mahaffie's dissenting opinion in *Reduced Pipeline Rates and Gathering Charges*, 243 ICC 115, 144–145 (1940).

128 *Celler Hearings* 455 (ICC Com'r Aitchison), 484, 485 (Chairman Clarke), 1957; Aitchison, *Some Observations Concerning Pipe Lines*, p. 236.

129 *O'Mahoney Report* 131 (1957).

130 Wolbert, *American Pipe Lines*, p. 21; Note, 102 U. Pa. L. Rev. 894, 907 (1954).

131 See Wolbert, *American Pipe Lines*, pp. 22–36, for discussion of technical problems involved in minimum tenders.

132 *Celler Hearings* 455 (Com'r Aitchison), 457 (Chairman Clarke), 1957; Aitchison, *Some Observations Concerning Pine Lines*, p. 236.

133 Rostow, *A National Policy For the Oil Industry* (1948), p. 63.

134 Att'y Gen., *Third Report* 55–56 (1958).

135 Webb, *ICC Regulation of the Oil Pipeline Industry* (Address Before the National Petroleum Association September 17, 1959), p. 7.

136 See note 118. For additional reference to reparation awards, see *Celler Hearings* 454 (1957) and Whitesel, *Recent Federal Regulation of the Petroleum Pipe Line as a Common Carrier*, 32 Corn. L. Q. 337, 369 (1947).

137 Webb, *ICC Regulation*, p. 7.

138 Sometimes a third issue — "independent" or "noncarrier gathering" — is discussed in conjunction with the unconnected well problem. See Att'y Gen., *Third Report* 79–86 (1958).

139 *O'Mahoney Report* 28–30 (1957); Att'y Gen., *Third Report* 70 (1958); *Wherry Report* 20 (1949); cf. Complaint, pp. 35–36, *United States* v. *American Petroleum Institute*, Civil No. 8524, D.D.C., September 30, 1940; *Col-Tex Refining Co.* v. *Railroad Comm.*, 150 Tex. 340, 240 S.W. 2d 747, 750 (1951).

140 *Texas Railroad Comm., General Inquiry Relative to Common Carriers of Crude Oil In Texas* (Hereinafter referred to as *Tex. Gen. Inquiry*), vol. I, pp. 52–53, 70, 90, 156, 214; vol. II, pp. 8, 19 (April 1 and 2, 1957); Rogers, *Common Purchaser, Market Demand, Pipeline Proration* in Southwestern Legal Foundation Ninth Annual Institute on Oil & Gas Law and Taxation 45, 75 (1958).

141 *Tex. Gen. Inquiry*, vol. I, pp. 7, 119; vol. II, pp. 65–66, 95–96 (May 13–15, 1957); *O'Mahoney Report* 129, 131 (1957); *Celler Hearings* 1168 (1957); cf. Wolbert, *American Pipe Lines*, p. 42.

142 *Celler Hearings* 1134 (1957); cf. Rostow & Sachs, *Entry into the Oil Refining Business*, p. 893; Cookenboo, *Crude Oil Pipe Lines*, p. 142.

143 *Celler Hearings* 1168 (1957).

144 Att'y Gen., *Second Report* 88 (1957); Rogers, *Common Purchaser*, p. 83.

145 *Celler Hearings* 1168 (1957).

146 *O'Mahoney Report* 28–31 (1957).

147 Att'y Gen., *Second Report* 94–101 (1957).
148 *Tex. Gen. Inquiry*, Pl. First Amended Petition 11 (1957).
149 *Ibid.*
150 *Tex. Gen. Inquiry*, Pl. Br. 21 (1957).
151 *Tex. Gen. Inquiry*, vol. I, pp. 52–53 (Geo. Mitchell); p. 70 (R. S. Anderson); p. 90 (E. L. Wilson); p. 156 (Geo. Livermore); p. 214 (Harvey Gandy); vol. II, pp. 8, 19 [Jack Boles] (April 1 and 2, 1957); Rogers, *Common Purchaser*, p. 75.
152 The Commission's order did not grant connections to the individuals concerned despite the fact that their situations were in evidence. *Tex. R.R. Comm., Oil & Gas Docket Nos. 108, et al.*, Order No. 20–38,015 (June 4, 1958).
153 *Ibid.* "Whereas, From evidence adduced at said hearing and from general knowledge of decreased demand, the Commission finds that as of the date of this order the capacity of trunk pipe lines in Texas is adequate . . . the request of Petitioners for an enlargement of common carrier pipe lines from West Texas to the Gulf Coast be and the same is hereby denied."
154 In any future case of request for connection, either the pipeline or the producer may bring the matter before the Commission and a hearing will be held on 10 days' notice. The Commission will consider, among other factors, the ability of the pipeline to transport the quality of oil involved, the market or lack of market for the tendered oil, and the period required to return the capital investment for the connection. *Tex. R.R. Comm., Oil & Gas Docket Nos. 108, et al.*, Order No. 20–38,015 (June 4, 1958).
155 The timing was as follows: *Tex. Gen. Inquiry*, Pl. First Amended Petition, filed in January, 1957; *Tex. Gen. Inquiry*, Order No. 20–34,913 (setting hearing and directing pipelines to show cause why they should not be ordered to offer connections to all wells requesting connection), issued Feb. 19, 1957; Appearances before O'Mahoney Committee on Feb. 28, 1957; *Tex. Gen. Inquiry*: Testimony received April 1–3, 1957, and May 13–15, 1957; Briefs filed Dec., 1957; Oral Argument, Jan., 1958; Decision (Order No. 20–38,015) issued June 4, 1958.
156 Att'y Gen., *Second Report* (1957) was released in October, 1957. Compare this with the dates of the Texas Railroad Commission proceeding shown in footnote 155.
157 *Tex. Gen. Inquiry*, Pl. Exh. 44; Rogers, *Common Purchaser*, p. 74.
158 In every Annual Report of the Oil & Gas Division from 1948 to 1958 the Texas Railroad Commission has reported the continued expansion of pipelines at a rate commensurate with the economic growth of the state, with the effect that every producing field of any size or significance was adequately and properly served. 1948 Annual Report of the Oil & Gas Division, Railroad Commission of Texas, p. 10; 1949 Annual Report, p. 8; 1950 Annual Report, p. 12; 1951 Annual Report, p. 12; 1952 Annual Report, p. 15; 1953 Annual Report, p. 15; 1954 Annual Report, p. 14; 1955 Annual Report, p. 13; 1956 Annual Report, p. 13; 1957 Annual Report, p. 12; 1958 Annual Report, p. 14.
159 Wolbert, *American Pipe Lines*, p. 10, n. 40; McLean & Haigh, *The Growth of Integrated Oil Companies*, pp. 187–188. For example, the 727-mile, 12-to-16-inch Four Corners Line, completed in 1958 cost around $50½ million.
160 Emerson, *Salient Characteristics of Petroleum Pipe Line Transportation*, p. 31 (70 per cent); Kinsolving, *Underground Rivers of Oil* (1954), p. 6 (80 per cent).
161 For example, the extension of the Prairie Pipe Line into the Ranger Field in Texas. *Brundred Bros. v. Prairie Pipe Line Co.*, 68 I.C.C. 458, 461 (1922). Another example is the Cumberland Pipe Line Co. formerly of the "Southern group" of pipelines. The Kentucky fields served by its gathering lines declined rapidly, operating revenues and return on investment dropped severely, causing sale of the property at considerably less than its depreciated value. *Oil Pipe Line Facts & Figures* (1933), p. 8.
162 Cookenboo, *Crude Oil Pipe Lines*, chap. I.
163 *Celler Hearings*, 1135 (1957), Mr. J. L. Burke testifying:
Service had a combination 12- and 16-inch line with many stations from the Rocky Mountain area to the midcontinent. It was on a route originally laid out in 1923. In 1950, a competitor — Platte Pipe Line Co. — announced, and in 1952 completed, a modern 20-inch line from the same origin to the same destination area.

Platte's initial tariffs published rates 9 cents per barrel lower than Service. It increased its capacity in 1953 and 1954. Service's calculations showed that the economies of its competitor's operation were such that, if it reached capacity, its rate to yield an 8-per cent return would be so low that Service could not recover its depreciation if it published a competitive rate.

Then a new 18- to 20-inch line was announced by Arapahoe Pipe Line Co., from the same origin area, with ability to reach the same destinations. Already flanked on one side, Service found itself in prospect of being surrounded. The alternatives were simple; build a new line, or quit. Service built a new 625-mile, 20-, 22-, 24-inch system with the highest potential volume and the lowest potential cost.

A vital factor in the calculated-risk decision was the hope of securing nonproprietary traffic. As soon as it announced construction, Service reduced rates to a competitive level. It has since, in 1957, initiated a further reduction.

See also *Tex. Gen. Inquiry*, vol. II, p. 199 (May 15, 1957).

[164] See footnote 163.

[165] Cookenboo, *Crude Oil Pipe Lines*, pp. 126–127; Wolbert, *American Pipe Lines*, p. 103; Beard, *Regulation of Pipe Lines as Common Carriers*, pp. 122–123; Dow, *The Issue of Pipe Line Divorcement* (1939), pp. 18–19; Mills, *The Pipe Line's Place in the Oil Industry* (1935), pp. 97–98; cf. Williamson & Daum, *The American Petroleum Industry; The Age of Illumination* (1957), p. 598.

[166] See Cook, *Control of the Petroleum Industry By Major Oil Companies* (TNEC Monograph No. 39, 1941), *passim*; Rostow, *A National Policy For the Oil Industry*, p. 11; *Wherry Report* 19 (1949); Rostow & Sachs, *Entry into the Oil Refining Business*, pp. 879–880; Att'y Gen., *First Report* 24 (1956); *Celler Report* 124–128 (1959); cf. Wolbert, *American Pipe Lines*, p. 9.

[167] The only comparable figures are on percentage of mileage.

Year	No. Co's.	No. Pipeline Co's.	Per cent Crude Mile	Per cent Product Mile	Source
1938	20	....	85.4	96.1	Cook, pp. 21, 37
1940	19	....	84.5	....	Cookenboo, p. 34
1946	16	51	84.0	....	Spal, 15 ICC Prac.J., p. 566
1948	19	....	88.2	....	Cookenboo, p. 35
1950	....	54	80.8	90.8	Att'y Gen. 1st Rep., p. 24
1958	20	89	70.7	95.7	Celler Report, p. 126

[168] Mason, *Workable Competition Versus Workable Monopoly* in N. Y. Bar Ass'n Antitrust Law Symposium 67, 69 (1951).

[169] Heflebower, *Economics of Size*, 24 U. Chi. Bus. J. 253, 266 (1951).

[170] Cookenboo, *Crude Oil Pipe Lines*, p. 37.

[171] Hamilton, *Competition in Oil* (1958), p. 42; Hale & Hale, *Market Power*, pp. 138, 199; cf. Att'y Gen. *Nat. Comm. Rep.* 326 (1955); Bork, *Vertical Integration*, p. 195.

[172] In addition to the long-distance pipelines discussed in the text, there is a plethora of gathering lines and short trunk lines, both crude and products, owned by so-called "independent" refiners. This has been true for a long time. These lines include *among others*: *Anderson-Prichard Oil Corporation*, through a subsidiary, owns approximately 100 miles of various size crude oil lines in Oklahoma and Kansas, supplying refineries at Cyril, Oklahoma, and Arkansas City, Kansas.

Bell Oil and Gas Company, either directly or through pipe line subsidiary, owns 200 miles of gathering lines in North Texas and South Oklahoma, serving its refinery at Grandfield, Oklahoma.

Ben Franklin Refining Company owns and operates 365 miles of gathering lines in Oklahoma, serving refinery at Ardmore, Oklahoma. The company also owns a short products line connecting its refinery to the Sinclair 8-inch Waco-Coffeyville line which, in turn, ties into Great Lakes near the Oklahoma-Kansas border.

Champlin Oil and Refining Company. 695 miles of gathering and trunk lines extending from various fields in Oklahoma to refinery at Enid, Oklahoma.

Clark Oil & Refining Corporation, products line connecting to Badger and Wolverine.

Crown Central Petroleum Corporation, through a subsidiary, owns and operates gathering lines in the Manvel area (Brazoria County, Texas) and trunk line from that area to refinery on Houston Ship Channel. Also owns and operates gathering lines in the Haskell district (Haskell County), the Cordele Field (Jackson County), and the Pierce Junction Field (Harris County), Texas.

Kendall Refining Company owns and operates 130 miles of gathering lines in the Bradford Field, delivering to its refinery at Bradford, Pennsylvania.

Kerr-McGee Oil Industries, Inc., owns and operates 1,550 miles of gathering and trunk lines, ranging from 2 inches to 10 inches in diameter. It also owns products lines connecting its refineries and tying into the Oklahoma-Mississippi River and Great Lakes lines.

Leonard Refineries, Inc., either directly or through subsidiaries owns and operates 835 miles of gathering lines from fields in Michigan to refineries at Alma and Mt. Pleasant, Michigan. It also owns a short products line from Alma to Lansing, Michigan.

Naph-Sol Refining Company owns and operates approximately 110 miles of line, serving fields in Michigan. (Refinery is located at Muskegon, Michigan.)

Premier Oil Refining Company of Texas owns and operates approximately 625 miles of lines in East Texas and West Central Texas, serving refineries at Long View, Baird, and Fort Worth, Texas.

[173] The prototype of this category is the 1879 Tide-Water line from Bradford to Williamsport, Pennsylvania — 108 miles of 6-inch. A modern example is the Plains Pipe Line — 380 miles of 4-inch to 8-inch crude trunk lines in eastern Wyoming, principally from Fiddler Creek to Lance Creek, Wyoming. The ultimate owner is Clint Murchison, Texas independent oil producer.

[174] *Independent Crude Line Joint Ventures with Majors:*

Line	Length	Size	Location	Ownership	Per cent
Butte	506	6–10–12–16 inch	Poplar, Mont., to Guernsey, Wyo.	Murphy	17.5
Four Corners	725	12–16 inch	Aneth, Utah & Bisti, New Mex., to Los Angeles	Superior	
Portland	332	12–18 inch	S. Portland, Me., to New Troy, Vt.	Canadian Petrofina	

[175] *Independent Crude Line Joint Ventures with Others:*

Line	Length	Size	Location	Ownership	Per cent
Minnesota	256	16 inch	Clearbrook to Pine Bend, Minnesota	Woodley Oil Southern Prod. Howard Marshall	40 40 20

[176] *Independent Refiner Crude Lines (wholly owned):*

Line	Length	Size	Location	Ownership
Jayhawk	242	10–12 inch	Mead, Kan., to McPherson & Wichita	Derby Refining - N.C.R.A.
Jayhawk	130	6 inch	Pheasant Prairie and Interstate to Mead	Derby Refining - N.C.R.A.
Mich.-Ohio	360	6–8 inch	Toledo, Ohio, to Midland, Michigan	Leonard
Valvoline P/L	255	3–4 inch	Warren, Pa., to Sugar Creek, W. Va.	Ashland
Valvoline P/L	43	6 inch	Douglas, Ind., to Owensboro, Ky.	Ashland

There is also the extensive network of lines owned by Ashland Oil & Refining Co., consisting of 1,160 miles in So. Illinois and Indiana; 740 miles in eastern Kentucky; 225 miles in western Kentucky; 1,000 miles in Pennsylvania and West Virginia and 242 miles in the Spraberry area of West Texas.

[177] *Independent Refiner Products Lines (wholly owned):*

Line	Length	Size	Location	Ownership
Apco Prod.	40	4 inch	Cyril, Okla., to Duncan, Okla.	Anderson - Pritchard
Ashland	235	8 inch	Freedom, Pa., to Findlay, Ohio	Ashland
Champlin	516	6 inch	Enid, Okla., to Rock Rapids, Iowa	Champlin
Champlin	139	6 inch	Enid, Okla., to Oklahoma City, Okla.	Champlin
Emerald	105	6 inch	Sunray, Tex., to Junct. with Okan Pipeline	Shamrock
Husky	100	10 inch	Cody, Wyo., to Billings (proposed)	Husky
Products P/L (LPG)	110	6 inch	Provident City to Texas City	Goliad Corp. (Wilcox)
Saal	110	6 inch	Lubbock, Tex., to Amarillo	Shamrock
West Emerald	297	6 inch	Amarillo, Tex., to Albuquerque, N. Mex.	Shamrock
Wyoming-Neb.	213	6 inch	Cheyenne, Wyo., to No. Platte, Neb.	Frontier

[178] *Independent Joint Venture with Majors — Crude Lines:*

Line	Length	Size	Location	Ownership	Per cent
Rancho	455	24 inch	McCamey to Houston	⎰ Ashland ⎱ Eastern Sts. ⎩ Crown Central	5–7 5–7 5–7
Tecumseh	201	20 inch	Griffith, Ind., to Cygnet, Ohio	Ashland	20

[179] *Independent Joint Venture with Majors — Products Lines:*

Line	Length	Size	Location	Ownership	Per cent
Bayou System	305	10 inch	Houston to Baton Rouge	⎰ Crown Central ⎱ Republic	8–12
Phillips-Shamrock	169	6 inch	McKae, Tex., to Denver	Shamrock	
Project Five (Recently bought by Texas Eastern)	150	10 inch	Eldorado to Helena, Arkansas	Premier of Texas	2
Yellowstone	538	10 inch	Billings to Spokane	Husky (Clack)	6

[180] *Railroads in the Pipeline Business:*

Name	Length	Size	Location	Ownership
So.Pac.P.L.	426	8 inch	El Paso to Phoenix	So. Pac. R.R.
So.Pac.P.L.	350	10–8–6 inch	Richmond (San Francisco) to Fallon, Nev.	So. Pac. R.R.

PIPELINE DIVORCEMENT 137

Name	Length	Size	Location	Ownership	
So.Pac.P.L.	418	12–16 inch	Los Angeles to Phoenix	So. Pac. R.R.	
Butte	506	6–10–12–16 inch	Poplar, Mont., to Guernsey, Wyo.	Northern Pacific	10

181 *Natural Gas Transmission Co's. in Pipeline Business:*

Name	Length	Size	Location	Ownership
El Paso Nat.	166	8–6 inch	Gallup, N. Mex., to Aneth, Utah (Products)	El Paso
El Paso Nat.	240	6 inch	El Paso to Odessa, Tex. (Products)	El Paso
El Paso Nat.	36	4 inch	Gallup to Prewitt, N. Mex. (Products)	El Paso
El Paso Nat.	90	6 inch	Gallup, N. Mex., to Blanco (Crude)	El Paso
El Paso Nat.	118	4 inch	Pettigrew, N. Mex., to Gallup, N. Mex. (Crude)	El Paso
Tex. Eastern	1180	16–20 inch	Houston to Moundsville W. Va. (Products)	Texas Eastern
Tex. Eastern	233	14 inch	Seymour, Ind., to Chicago (Products)	Texas Eastern

182 *Chemical Firms in the Pipeline Business:*

Name	Length	Size	Location	Ownership	
Trust & River	250	6 inch	Big Spring, Tex., to Duncan, Okla. (Products)	Cosden	
Conn. Pipeline (Proposed)	62	12 inch	New Haven to Springfield, Mass. (Products)	Olin Mathison	
Project Five (now Texas East)	150	10 inch	Eldorado to Helena, Ark. (Products)	Monsanto (Lion Oil Co.)	5

183 *Independent Common Carrier Crude Pipelines:*

Name	Length	Size	Location
Belle Fourche Pipe Line	31	6 inch	Donkey Creek to Fiddler Creek, Wyo.
Buckeye Pipeline	662	6–8–12 inch	Griffith, Ind. to Buffalo via Northern & New York Transit
Buckeye Pipeline	98	2/8 inch	Lima to Toledo
Buckeye Pipeline	37	8 inch	Cygnet to Sylvania, Ohio
Buckeye Pipeline	157	8–12 inch	Cygnet to Cleveland
Buckeye Pipeline	42	8 inch	Hazel Junction, Ohio, to Trenton, Mich.
Buckeye Pipeline	29	6 inch	Mantua to Cleveland
Eureka	159	3/6 inch	Morgantown, W. Va., to Charleston, W. Va.
National Transit	77	6 inch	Cooks Ferry, Pa., to Morgantown, W. Va.
National Transit	130	6 inch	Nedsky to Duke, Pa.
National Transit	15	6 inch	Chester to Philadelphia
Powder River	104	4–6 inch	Sumatra to Billings, Mont.

184 *Independent Common Carrier Products Pipelines:*

Name	Length	Size	Location
Augusta	46	8 inch	Arkansas City, Kan., to Augusta, Kan.
Buckeye	366	8 inch	Lawrenceville, Ill., to Toledo
	76	8 inch	Lima to Columbus
	70	8 inch	Wayne, Mich., to Flint, Mich.
	187	8 inch	Griffith, Ind., to Lima, Ohio
	173	8 inch	Toledo to Cleveland
	409	10–14–16 inch	Linden, N. J., to Utica and Caledonia, N. Y.
	72	8 inch	Mantua to Cooks Ferry, Pa.
Kaneb	198	10 inch	Wichita, Kan., to Fairmont, Neb.
	100	6 inch	Phillipsburg, Kan., to Fairmont, Neb.
	155	6 inch	Fairmont, Neb., to Yankton, S. D.
Nat'l. Transit	68	6–8 inch	Pittsburgh to Morgantown, W. Va.
Southern	291	2/6–8 inch	Morgantown, W. Va. to Marcus Hook, Pa.

185 *Cooperatives in the Crude Pipeline Business:*

(1) Coop. Ref. Ass'n. — 102 — 6 inch — Holdrege, Neb., to Bemis, Kansas

(2) Indiana Farm Bureau Coop. Ass'n. owns and operates 400 miles of 2–3–4″ lines **in the** Illinois basin serving Mt. Vernon, Ind. refinery.

(3) Nat'l Coop.

Ref. Ass'n.	121	8 inch	Valley Center to Coffeeville, Kansas
Nat'l Coop. Ref. Ass'n.	52	8 inch	Ramsey, Okla., to Caney, Kan.

Name	Length	Size	Location	Ownership	Per cent
Ind. Farm Bureau	224	8 inch	Mt. Vernon, Ind., to Peru, Ind.	Ind. Farm Bureau	..
National Coop. Ref. Ass'n.	225	6 inch	McPherson, Kan., to Omaha & Council Bluffs	National Coop.	..
Oil Basin P.L.	230	8 inch	Billings & Laurel to Glendive, Mont.	Farmers Union Central Exch.	35

[187] Att'y Gen., *Third Report* 49 (1958), citing U. S. Bureau of Corporations, Report of the Commissioner of Corporations on the Petroleum Industry, Part 1 (1907), pp. 213–214.

[188] Interstate Commerce Commission, Transport Statistics in the United States, Part 6 (1958), pp. 10, 13. These figures represent lines reporting to the ICC. The over-all figures as of December 31, 1958, are: 70,317 miles crude trunk lines; 75,182 miles of crude gathering lines, for a total of 145,499 miles of crude lines; there were 44,483 miles of products pipelines on that date, hence, the grand total of pipeline mileage as of December 31, 1958, was 189,982 miles. See *Oil Daily*, Jan. 11, 1960, p. 8.

[189] *Ibid.*, p. 4.

[190] *Oil Pipe Line Facts & Figures*, p. 3.

[191] Att'y Gen., *Third Report* 46 (1958).

[192] *Ibid.*, pp. 49–50.

[193] Bond, *Oil Pipelines*, p. 730.

[194] *Ibid.*, p. 741.

[195] Att'y Gen., *Third Report* 73–74 (1958).

[196] See notes 108–112.

[197] Butte Pipe Line Co., ICC No. 65 (March 2, 1958).

[198] *Route 1*: Butte Pipe Line Company to Ft. Laramie, Goshen County, Wyoming; Service Pipe Line Company to Wood River, Madison County, Illinois; The Ohio Oil Company to Lima, Allen County, Ohio; The Buckeye Pipe Line Company to Ohio-Pennsylvania state line; Northern Pipe Line Company to Bear Creek, Armstrong County, Pennsylvania; Northern Pipe Line Company and National Transit Company to Pennsylvania-New York state line; thence via New York Transit Company to destination.

Route 2: Butte Pipe Line Company to Ft. Laramie, Goshen County, Wyoming; Service Pipe Line Company to Hart Junction, Lake County, Indiana; Tecumseh Pipe Line Company to Cygnet, Wood County, Ohio; The Buckeye Pipe Line Company to Ohio-Pennsylvania state line; Northern Pipe Line Company to Bear Creek, Armstrong County, Pennsylvania; Northern Pipe Line Company and National Transit Company to Pennsylvania-New York state line; thence via New York Transit Company to destination.

[199] In addition, these 48 carriers reported participation in 1,637 joint tariffs published by others. This figure cannot be used as a yardstick, because it obviously involves duplication. However, it has utility as a trend indicator.

[200] Four Corners, Muskegon, Salt Lake, Sun of Illinois, and Suntide. Powder River is a small line from Montana fields to Billings and posts only two local tariffs.

[201] Portland (Portland, Me., to Canadian border connection with Montreal Pipe Line Co.) and Trans-Mountain (from a border connection with a Canadian affiliate, to the Seattle area).

[202] Calculated from Interstate Commerce Commission, Transport Statistics in the United States, Part 6 (1958), pp. 12–13.

[203] Att'y Gen., *Third Report* 74 (1958).

[204] For example, a movement of crude tendered to Shell Pipe Line Corp. at Jal, New Mexico, for Wood River, Illinois, would be transported by Shell Pipe Line through its space in the Basin and Ozark systems but the movement would be Shell Pipe Line throughout and the physical transfer would not show in the ICC figures.

[205] Att'y Gen., *Third Report* 75 (1958).

[206] *Ibid.*, pp. 79, 87.

[207] Cf. Thompson, *Recent Steps in Government Regulation of Business*, 28 Corn. L. Q. 1, 14 (1942).

[208] *Celler Hearings* 1134 (1957).

[209] Att'y Gen., *Third Report* 49 (1958).

[210] *Celler Hearings* 1134 (1957). Typical of the state of knowledge of that period is the fact that a cost study published in 1934 ignored lines larger than 12 inches in diameter. Young, "Applied Design and Economics of Pipe Lines," *Oil & Gas Journal* (Nov. 8, 1934), pp. 38, 41, cited by Cookenboo, *Crude Oil Pipe Lines and Competition in the Oil Industry*, p. 136.

[211] A technical paper delivered before the American Institute of Mining & Metallurgical Engineers in 1942 expounded upon the subject and espoused the economies of 24-inch lines. Hill, "Engineering Economics of Long Petroleum Pipe Lines," in *Petroleum Development & Technology* (1942), pp. 231, 233–234.

[212] Cookenboo, *Crude Oil Pipe Lines and Competition in the Oil Industry*, p. 138.

[213] The first "big inch" line was constructed by Stanolind (Service) Pipe Line in

1944. This 385 mile 16-inch line ran from the Slaughter field in the Permian Basin of West Texas to Drumright, Oklahoma. *A Primer of Oil Pipe Line Operation*, p. 114 (Bulletin issued by Petroleum Extension Service, University of Texas, 1953). It proved the practicability of "big inch" long lines.

[214] *Celler Hearings* 1134–1135 (1957); Att'y Gen., *Fourth Report* 26, 46 (1959).

[215] *A Primer of Oil Pipe Line Operation*, p. 114.

[216] Kinsolving, *Underground Rivers of Oil*, p. 5. Another important development of this era was the manufacture of pumping equipment with the requisite capacity.

[217] *Celler Hearings* 1135 (1957); cf. Cookenboo, *Crude Oil Pipe Lines and Competition in the Oil Industry*, pp. 20–22; U. S. Dept. of Commerce, Industry Report, Domestic Transportation, Petroleum Transportation 28 (Jan.–Mar., 1949).

[218] *Celler Hearings* 1135 (1957); McLean & Haigh, *The Growth of Integrated Oil Companies*, pp. 187–188.

[219] For example, 24-inch costs $70,000 per mile as opposed to $50,000 for 18-inch, a 40 per cent increase in cost, but the capacity is double.

[220] Cookenboo, *Crude Oil Pipe Lines and Competition in the Oil Industry*, chap. I; U. S. Dept. of Commerce, Industry Report — Domestic Transportation Petroleum Transportation 28 (Jan.–Mar., 1949).

[221] *A Primer of Oil Pipe Line Operation*, p. 115.

[222] Among these lines were:

Year	Company	Origin and Destination	Size	Length
1947	Service	Humboldt, Kan., to Manhattan, Ill.	20 inch	475 mi.
1948	Magnolia	Corsicana, Tex., to Patoka, Ill.	20 inch	648 mi.
1949	Basin	Jal, New Mex., to Cushing, Okla.	20–22–24 inch	516 mi.
	Ozark	Cushing, Okla., to Wood River, Ill.	22 inch	433 mi.
1950	Mid-Valley	Longview Tex., to Lima, Ohio	20–22 inch	1053 mi.
1952	Platte	Welch, Wyo., to Wood River, Ill.	20 inch	1080 mi.
	Sinclair	Drumright, Okla., to Chicago, Ill.	22–24 inch	675 mi.
1952	Ohio	Wood River, Ill., to Lima, Ohio	20–22 inch	362 mi.
1953	West Tex. Gulf	Colorado City to Nederland, Tex.	26 inch	465 mi.
	West Tex. Gulf	Wortham to Longview, Tex.	20 inch	112 mi.
	Rancho	McCamey to Houston, Tex.	24 inch	457 mi.
	Lakehead	Superior, Wis., to Sarnia, Ont.	30 inch	645 mi.
1954	Service	Ft. Laramie, Wyo., to Freeman, Mo.	20–24 inch	625 mi.
	Arapahoe	Merino, Colo., to Humboldt, Kan.	18–20 inch	494 mi.
1955	Butte	Poplar, Mont., to Guernsey, Wyo.	10–16 inch	419 mi.
1957	Tecumseh	Griffith, Ind., to Cygnet, Ohio	20 inch	201 mi.
1958	Tex.-N. Mex.	Aneth, Utah, to Jal, New Mex.	16 inch	512 mi.
	Sinclair	Mexia to Houston, Tex.	20 inch	150 mi.
	Four Corners	Aneth, Utah, to Los Angeles	12–16 inch	725 mi.

[223] A.P.I. *Petroleum Facts and Figures* (12th ed. 1956), p. 242; Att'y Gen., *Third Report* 49 (1958).

[224] *A Primer of Oil Pipe Line Operation*, p. 119; Att'y Gen., *Third Report* 75–79 (1958).

[225] *Celler Hearings* 1135 (1957); cf. McLean & Haigh, *The Growth of Integrated Oil Companies*, p. 224.

[226] Att'y Gen., *Third Report* 77 (1958).

[227] Att'y Gen., *Fourth Report* 26 (1959) states:
"Among these PAW projects [pipelines built specifically to join previous separate lines into a national network] was construction of the first of the large 'undivided interest' trunk pipelines, a highly significant feature in pipeline development." This has reference to the Bayou System which was the archetype of the undivided interest line.

[228] Att'y Gen., *Third Report* 77–78 (1958).

[229] *A Primer of Oil Pipe Line Operation*, pp. 119–120.

[230] *Ibid.*, p. 120; Att'y Gen., *Third Report* 78 (1958).

[231] Att'y Gen., *Third Report* 78 (1958).

[232] *Ibid.*, p. 77, n. 251.

[233] The shares of these, and the other participants in the Rancho System are listed in Att'y Gen., *Third Report* 77 (1958).

Changes Under Law

The Sherman Act and the Oil Industry

by Simon N. Whitney

FEDERAL TRADE COMMISSION

I regret that I am not authorized to expound and defend the policy of the antitrust enforcement agencies, as has been suggested here. The opinions I express will be my own, drawn largely from a study I made before joining the staff of the Federal Trade Commission. At the Commission I have not participated in any petroleum litigation.

My remarks will not be strictly confined to the Sherman Antitrust Act. The other important antitrust laws are closely connected with this fundamental statute: thus anything which violates Section 1 of the Sherman Act probably also violates Section 5 of the Federal Trade Commission Act; and cases can be brought under both 1 of the Sherman Act and 3 of the Clayton Act, or 2 of the Sherman Act and 7 of the Clayton Act. Of the state antitrust laws and suits, on the other hand, I shall not speak — though there were many against the old Standard Oil combination,[1] and Texas, Michigan, Wisconsin and other states have shown some activity in recent years.

The discussion of antitrust cases by several previous speakers has made it easier for me to keep within my 20 minutes. It has also constituted a recognition of the importance of the antitrust laws in the development of the petroleum industry. Those laws have had a similar influence throughout most of the economy. I concede that several other features of the economy are more important in explaining its prosperity and productivity — for example, the aggressive character of the typical American and hence the American businessman, the national propensity to produce and reinvest wealth, and even Yankee ingenuity (not to mention our huge market and our rich raw materials, including oil). But to me, as to most other students, the antitrust laws have seemed to offer a strong support to the individualism which was inherent in our pioneering environment, and a bulwark against the temptation to take refuge in cartels and restrictionism. Both the profit motive and the competitive spirit have contributed to the making of American industry. I think the earlier speakers would agree with this generalization, whatever reservations they may have (and we all have them) with respect to particular antitrust cases.

An industry is inevitably influenced by the mere existence of the antitrust laws, as it is by important antitrust precedents in other industries. Petroleum is no exception: the United States Steel decision of 1920, the Trenton Potteries decision of 1927, or the several patent cases of the late 1940's are merely a few of the many cases in other industries that have influenced the development of the oil industry. Petroleum has had its full share of cases: the chief of the antitrust division in 1951 was hardly exaggerating when he said that its "major battles historically and daily have been against the oil industry." His successor in 1957 remarked that 25 per cent of his lawyers (i.e., 70 or 75) were working on oil "prosecutions."

The most famous antitrust decision in petroleum, and possibly the most famous in any industry, is that in which Standard Oil Company of New Jersey was dissolved into 34 units in 1911.[2] Although there was little practical effect at first in the markets for crude oil and oil products, this was soon changed. The dissolution of a modern corporation (such as Standard was in 1911) almost

[1] Ralph W. and Muriel E. Hidy, *Pioneering in Big Business, 1882–1911* (New York, 1955), p. 683.
[2] *Standard Oil Co. of N. J.* v. *U. S.*, 221 U.S. 1 (1911).

inevitably creates successor companies of a less integrated character. They seek, therefore, to round out their operations, just as they seek to achieve a larger size than that in which the dissolution left them. The Standard successor companies began to move into each other's territories within half a dozen years, and mergers took place among them and with other companies designed to restore in some degree the geographically diversified and vertically integrated character of the old combination.

Henrietta Larson, followed by other speakers here, emphasized the declining share of Standard Oil in the refining industry before 1911. From their statistics, it is clear that, even without the 1911 dissolution, there would have been no monopoly in petroleum. The share of the Standard company in total refining would probably be about the 40 per cent or so that the successor companies have today. An undissolved company might, if anything, have been less aggressive in maintaining its share of the market. The fact that the cracking process was not perfected until the break-up of the combination, enabling its originators to get help from their own successor company, may be indicative in this connection.[3] We would, therefore, without the dissolution, have an industry in which the principal company would have a share of the market somewhat larger than United States Steel's share in steel, though less than General Motors' share in automobiles. That would not be an unusual structure — but I believe the petroleum structure is healthier as it is.

The next antitrust case of any significance permitted suppliers to win or hold the custom of service stations by leasing tanks or pumps to the dealer on condition that these be used for the suppliers' products only.[4] Supplying facilities was thus approved as a way of setting customers up in business and, by the same token, of conducting competition. Two Federal Trade Commission complaints have challenged the practice as a competitive method, though not as a way of establishing new customers. At the Hearing Examiner level, the respondents were cleared earlier this year (1959).[5]

The next antitrust case worthy of mention permitted two Standard successor companies, Socony and Vacuum, to merge, thus giving a green light to the mergers that were rounding out petroleum corporations geographically and operationally.[6] Since 1950 we have

[3] Paul H. Giddens, *Standard Oil Company (Indiana): Oil Pioneer of the Middle West* (New York, 1955), p. 149.
[4] *FTC* v. *Sinclair Refining Co.*, 261 U.S. 463 (1923).
[5] FTC Docket 6915, Socony Mobil Oil Co., and 7044, Shell Oil Co.
[6] *U. S.* v. *Standard Oil Co. of N. J.*, 47 Fed. 2d 288 (E.D. Mo. 1931).

a new and stricter merger law — the amended Section 7 of the Clayton Act. It has been applied informally by the Department of Justice to block the proposed Texaco-Superior merger, and the Federal Trade Commission is trying to do the same with Gulf and Warren Petroleum.

I would like to offer a comment at this point. The country may find itself with the alternatives of seeing even more small business firms sell out to their larger competitors or of enforcing antimerger regulations which would be least liked by the small firms mentioned. The owner of a successful, closely held business will, as soon as age begins to make security seem preferable to further vigorous business activity, be tempted to sell to some large corporation with publicly held stock for which there is a ready market. A corporation in his own line of business is the most likely buyer, although a corporation in another industry may thus diversify into this one. If the son or son-in-law of the owner wants to carry on the business, the outcome may be different — unless prospect of inheritance taxes forces the sale even in this case.

John Enos has discussed the cracking patents decision,[7] and I need merely register agreement with his emphasis on the shift from competitive to cooperative use of patents. The influence of the antitrust laws, incidentally, helped create the whole patent pool — if the reluctance of Standard of New Jersey to maintain its patent right to the full, and thus perhaps deal a very serious blow to The Texas Company, was influenced by a fear of later antitrust action.[8] The cracking decision, incidentally, like the ones dealing with equipment leasing and the Socony-Vacuum merger, might not (though I do not say "would not") have the same outcome under today's conditions.

One of the most painful antitrust memories of the oil industry is that which eventuated in the epochal Socony-Vacuum decision of the Supreme Court in 1940, which ruled that the buying programs for "distress gasoline" operated in the Midcontinent area — and, for that matter, in California as well — were unlawful since they constituted concerted action "for the purpose and with the effect" of influencing prices.[9] One may sympathize with the feelings of industry members who had received the blessing of the then duly constituted federal authorities (under the National Recovery Administration), only to be indicted, brought into court for three

[7] *Standard Oil Co. (Ind.)* v. *U. S.*, 283 U.S. 163 (1931).
[8] George Sweet Gibb and Evelyn H. Knowlton, *The Resurgent Years, 1911–1927* (New York, 1956), p. 553.
[9] *U. S.* v. *Socony-Vacuum Oil Co.*, 310 U.S. 150 (1940).

months of 1937 in the city of Madison, and fined for their actions. One may recognize that concerted action temporarily supporting an industry segment which is in distress and engaged in cutthroat competition can be constructive in preventing abandonment of plant, and scattering of skilled personnel that will be needed again. But it seems in retrospect a sound precedent either to outlaw such programs generally, because of the danger of abuse and the difficulty the courts would have in passing on each case, or at least not to leave their operation in the hands of competitors with their own interest to serve.

In any event, the buying programs were halted, and many of the refineries that had been supported by those programs soon passed out of existence as a result of inadequate facilities in technology and marketing. The antitrust case merely speeded their fate by a little.

I shall now touch lightly on several cases of only slightly lesser fame. The Supreme Court's decision in the Ethyl case was significant chiefly in making it easier for the cut-rate elements in the industry to improve the quality of their gasoline.[10] It did not, of course, succeed in ending the policy of a premium price for "ethyl," since this policy was to the interest of manufacturer, refiners, and distributors alike.

I see no reason not to follow George Wolbert, the previous speaker, in his view that the pipeline consent decree [11] was less important than Interstate Commerce Commission action in reducing pipeline charges.

The Standard Oil-I.G. Farben consent decree was briefly reviewed earlier by Wallace Pratt.[12] His points that Standard of New Jersey received from its German connection technical information which later proved of great value, and that the facts were not correctly portrayed in a quick, wartime antitrust action, are quite reasonable and relevant. The case, however, has significance, along with some in the chemical industry, in pointing to the principle that agreements to interchange such information between a leading company here and a leading company abroad must not be too sweeping and exclusive in character.

We have just seen the end of what might have turned into an important venture in antitrust interpretation. In 1940 the Department of Justice filed its "Mother Hubbard" complaint against the principal industry trade association and 366 oil companies or sub-

[10] *Ethyl Gasoline Corp.* v. *U. S.*, 309 U.S. 436 (1940).
[11] *U. S.* v. *Atlantic Refining Co.*, Civil 14060 (Dist. of Col., 1941).
[12] *U. S.* v. *Standard Oil Co* (*N.J.*), Civil 2091 (Dist. of N.J., 1943).

sidiaries.[13] In 1950 it switched over to a suit against the seven leading companies on the West Coast, asking, among other remedies, for complete divorcement of all marketing operations. In a consent decree, which came nine years and one month later, the companies agreed to desist from unfair practices which they still denied and the Department of Justice still maintained that they had committed, but which in any event it seems desirable to avoid. The outcome of this suit should prove satisfactory to all.[14]

Another equally prolonged case has now been completed, unless the Congress takes a hand. The Federal Trade Commission lost, in the Supreme Court, its second attempt to prove that Standard of Indiana was not meeting competition in good faith when it gave low prices to certain large wholesaler-retailer customers in the Detroit area in the late 1930's.[15] On this issue — whether a company meeting a competitor's lower price offer to some customers should have to make a general price cut — it always seemed to me that either outcome (i.e., whether Congress eventually passes "S. 11" or not) might hurt the legitimate interests of one or another type of competitor.

The first antitrust case filed in the petroleum industry after World War II that reached the Supreme Court was one whose importance is hard to judge. It was brought under both the Sherman and Clayton acts, but decided under the Clayton Act (Section 3). The oil companies were told that if they sold a substantial amount of merchandise, they lost thereby the right to require that their dealers not handle competing products.[16] So far as I can tell, this decision and a companion one which followed it almost automatically, also from California,[17] had by 1956 somewhat (though not completely) eased the work of salesmen for smaller refiners in placing their products in service stations representing major companies. Reference is to the minor products rather than gasoline, since the split pump station is likely to remain a rarity for practical reasons.

Exclusive dealing is likely to remain a difficult question for a long time. The Department of Justice has just won a case against one of the companies operating in the East.[18] The Federal Trade Commission has several complaints pending against oil refiners and rubber manufacturers, alleging that the over-ride sales commissions

13 *U. S.* v. *American Petroleum Institute*, Civil 8524 (Dist. of Col., 1940).
14 *U. S.* v. *Standard Oil Co. of Calif.*, Civil 11584–C (S.D. Calif., 1959). Divorcement was not included in the consent decree.
15 *Standard Oil Co.* v. *FTC*, 340 U.S. 231 (1951); *FTC* v. *Standard Oil Co.*, 355 U.S. 396 (1958).
16 *Standard Oil Co. of Calif.* v. *U.S.*, 337 U.S. 293 (1949).
17 *Richfield Oil Corp.* v. *U. S.*, 343 U.S. 522 (1952).
18 *U. S.* v. *Sun Oil Co.*, 176 Fed. Supp. 715 (E.D. Pa., 1959).

paid by the latter to the former caused the oil refiners to put pressure on their dealers to handle the products of those rubber companies.[19]

There are too many current cases to permit discussion, and their status forbids discussion in any event. I shall list those (not mentioned above) which have come to my attention and which no doubt comprise nearly all of the current cases.

The Department of Justice has in recent years enjoined two or three local agreements designed to end gasoline price wars. It is currently charging (1) that the five companies which first penetrated the Middle East have operated a cartel; (2) that the requirements contract between Esso Standard and Standard of Kentucky involves an exclusive territory agreement; (3) that gasoline price wars in Boston and South Bend were concluded by price-fixing; and (4) that 22 large companies raised crude oil and product prices in collusion under cover of the Suez crisis.

The Federal Trade Commission, besides having completed one or two cases on discriminatory pricing in recent years, is now charging refiners with various actions (in particular, undue price-cutting, discriminatory subsidies, resale price maintenance, and suggesting appropriate differentials between prices for national and local brands of gasoline) in connection with gasoline price wars in various localities in the South and Middle West. It is evident that neither the economics nor the law of gasoline price wars, or of differentials between national and local brands, has found a satisfactory solution.

To summarize, antitrust cases have helped shape the oil industry as it is today. For example, such cases have assailed single-company domination and all price agreements, but they have permitted, and in a sense contributed to, the establishment of large integrated corporations. Even if some antitrust cases were wrongly conceived or executed,[20] they have served the well-known gadfly function. It is probably better to err — if error has occurred — on the side of too strict than too lax protection for a competitive economy.

[19] FTC Dockets 6485–6487.
[20] See Harold Fleming's critique of cases in *Ten Thousand Commandments: A Story of the Antitrust Laws* (New York, 1951).